WOMEN AND IDENTITY in Literature

WOMEN AND IDENTITY in Literature

Edited By

Shikha Sharma

AUTHORSPRESS

Worldwide Circulation through Authorspress Global Network
First Published in 2022
by
Authorspress
Q-2A Hauz Khas Enclave, New Delhi-110 016 (India)
Phone: (0) 9818049852
E-mail: authorspressgroup@gmail.com
Website: www.authorspressbooks.com

Women and Identity in Literature
ISBN 978-93-5529-162-2

Printed in India at Kensington Press

Preface

This book *Women and Identity in Literature* is a manifestation of women's identities in a male-oriented society, as they have always been labelled as 'inferior and vulnerable'. This is a collection of various chapters contributed by scholars and professors from different states and that will help in better understanding of the concept as this would have various perspectives belonging to different backgrounds. It is an attempt to talk about women, their empowerment and their status in today's society. This book also deals with the idea that how gender-roles are evolving and they are shattering the specified stereotyped norms and traditions. Women's endeavours to resist against gender specified identities and how they become irrelevant in modern or civilised society. It is having chapters related to the various themes which is an effort to raise voices for those who are still yearning to gain freedom and access to basic amenities.

My heartfelt thanks go to my publisher Authorspress, New Delhi, for believing in me and agreed to publish my edited book *Women and Identity in Literature*.

June 2022 **Shikha Sharma**

Contents

Introduction

"Have you ever felt inferior to others?"

This is something that happens in everyone's family between siblings. Because they have to share everything with each other, and the younger sibling has to face this when he/she has to carry on the things left by the elder one. This is just an example to illustrate the situations of marginalised women because when one can feel envy in his/her house having access to everything, then what could be the conditions of women who have been deprived of basic necessities also? We, as readers, need to raise our voices against the exploitation of women. Hence, one cannot deny the fact that now the situation or matter is not the same as before because the people have become more civilised and educated, but still, there are gaps where these formulated amendments for women are not applicable. Most of us know how a person might react when questioned about its identity and existence, because identity is the self-realisation of a person's existence. But when the same identity is being scrutinised by the so-called ideologists, then everything comes to an end. This is the similar case of women in our society who are always being questioned. However, the circumstances are gradually changing. Gender-specific characteristics are not imposed on members of a society, nor are they compelled to act in a certain way; rather, they are free to do so. One can notice the reconstruction of a society where identities are swapped as women are taking up the masculine attributes. For example, a single mother is taking up the responsibilities of both a mother and a father, a widow too does the duties of both parents at the same time, which indicates the changing attitude of people towards these women. Finally, it cannot be denied that, in some areas, women still yearn to reclaim their identities and be treated differently than mere vulnerable, inferior, child-bearers, and so on.

This book is an attempt to talk about the oppressed women who are marginalised in a male-oriented society. This present book can be a way to resist the prevalent stereotypical norms and traditions where some women are bearers of multi-marginalisation. Have you ever thought about it?

"Why do certain groups perform better than other groups?"

This is the exact state of women in a male-oriented society where they are not given equal opportunities as men. Hence, it becomes a reason for the downfall of women and their damnation. As members of modern society, we are aware that now the situations are getting better day by day, but there is still a loophole in making women empowered and independent because we know that somewhere, there are fragments of women who are still facing this discrimination and subjugation like tribal women, rural women, illiterate women, etc. This book is just a medium to raise voices and awareness for these women, and this is something that can be done for them to be an equal partner in the formulation of this society. The prominent idea is to smash these specified gender-roles and identities, and this can be achieved if women are also given an equal chance to engage in the development of a society. This is because men and women/male and female are like two sides of a coin which are interrelated. In the same manner, one cannot ignore the importance of the other as women also play an important role in the formulation of a civilised society. It is the need of the hour to understand that the purpose of writing this book is not to make people empathise with oppressed women, but rather, to provide them with equal access which can help them out in leading a successful life.

This book is a result of contributions made by scholars and professors from various fields, making it a dream come true for me. This would provide multiple approaches to looking at serious concerns related to women, as this is not a new area of research, but the collection of papers included in this book is something which might provide a new direction to this field.

So, it is a culmination of numerous Chapters based on various themes which talk in favour of women empowerment and access to education.

Shikha Sharma

CHAPTER 1

Reconstruction of Gender-Roles and Identities: A Study of Rabindranath Tagore's Select Short Stories

Shikha Sharma

Abstract

Feminism is something that must be known to most of us in today's world, but there are still some gaps in understanding the concepts of femininity and masculinity. The purpose is to understand the idea of identity and how it affects one's personality with changing traits of genders. The current paper is going to deal with changes in gender roles and how they have evolved over the period of time through exploring the short-stories by Rabindranath Tagore. The main focus would be on how gender-roles have changed and how men and women present themselves in today's socially constructed society. Gender-roles expect its people to behave in a specific way according to their sex, which is now being questioned in contemporary society because both men and women are exchanging their assigned duties.

Keywords: Feminism, Femininity, Masculinity, Gender-roles, Sex, Identity.

Introduction

Rabindranath Tagore is best known for his contribution to literature as he was a renowned novelist, a poet, an educator and a philosopher. He is known as India's literary titan, and he made contributions in the field of short stories. The paper broadcasts the set ideologies of a society and how it desires the people to act accordingly. Society plays a pivotal role in the construction of gender-roles, as there is a famous adage proclaiming the fact that gender is a social construction rather than biological. It is believed that God has created human beings and assigned them duties which best suit their sex respectively, such as, breadwinner, protector, superior, etc for male whereas, housewife, giver, submissive, inferior for females. This set hierarchy of power in a male-oriented society has been questioned in the prevalent era, where in contrary, women are taking up the responsibilities of the male sex. Identity is something which distinguishes one person from another and now in modern times these specified identities are gradually changing. Identity is representation of one's existence either of a person, class, community, gender, nation or race. The short-stories selected for this paper are "The Notebook and The Wife's Letter" and through these stories, the writer is trying to question about the notions that prevailed at that time and how the protagonists (women characters) in the stories fight against male hegemony and free themselves from the clutches of societal norms and conditions. They develop their own identity in the society. Hence, the ideal purpose is to see whether this gender-construction works to sustain male dominance or whether it has changed drastically.

The situation is yet to be completely changed because many people still adhere to old norms, traditions, and ideas that force them to behave in a certain way solely identified with their genders and identities. Hence, these gender-specific identities become irrelevant in modern or civilised society, as it can be witnessed nowadays that every individual prefers to do things that please him/her. This gender-role construction has developed over a period of time and is not based on natural human behavior.

Tagore's Short-Stories: The Wife's Letter and The Notebook

Tagore wrote about a male-oriented society where his female characters fought against all odds and shattered all the stereotypes of being forgivers, vulnerable, fragile, etc. In lieu of their bold acts, they suffer backlash at the hands of their family members, even their husbands too. In 'The Notebook', Uma is shown as having a passionate love for reading and writing as she had developed this habit of reading and writing after getting fascinated by her brother's writing, who is also a writer. She shares a special bond with her notebook, which is denoted as "prized possession" and was gifted to her by her brother to obliterate her pain. This short-story portrays the revolting spirit of Uma, who has a zeal to do something in life, whereas, on the other hand, her sisters-in-law leave no chance to make her feel embarrassed in front of the entire family. This indicates that not only men-to-women relationships are complex, but women-to-women too face complicated relationships in their lives.

This is not entirely a new concept where people talk about equality in the society. Ages before, Tagore had written about the need for equality, education, freedom, and access to the outer world through the projection of his female characters in his short-stories. Uma, a 9-year-old girl, is getting married, and her mother advises her, saying, "Do pay attention to the words of your mother-in-law, dear. Please carry on all your household chores and forget about reading and writing, "(Tagore). Instead of encouraging her, her mother restricts her from doing anything which is masculine in nature and binds her in promises of doing things what a woman ought to do. Because she is a woman, she is expected to be bound by only those characteristics associated with the female sex. Her husband, Pyarimohan, tried to ignore his wife's acts, but societal pressure forced him to teach her a lesson as if she had committed a crime or sin.

In another story, "The Wife's Letter", two characters are paradoxical in nature, i.e., Mrinal and Bindu. The former is shown as fierce, bold, and benevolent in nature. On the other hand, the latter is depicted as the most degraded/unexpected thing or object any family could ever have. "Inessential rubbish can easily find a place around our house, because people forget it, but an inessential girl is in the first place unwanted, and moreover impossible to overlook. Here she does not find a place even in the rubbish-heap" (210). It shows society's attitude towards an orphaned child (girl) where she always faces multiple discriminations such as being ugly (not meeting the set standards of being beautiful), unwanted, orphan, and most prominently, a woman. She is inessential, yet this status makes her so essential in society's stare. As Simone de Beauvoir said, "one is not born a woman, but rather becomes a woman". Bindu surrenders in front of these stereotyped ideologies instead of fighting against them, and here she herself decides to become a woman who is always treated as inferior and vulnerable in society. There is no biological, psychological, or economic destiny that defines the figure that the human female acquires in society; it is civilisation as a whole that develops this product, intermediate between female and eunuch, that is referred to as feminine. It is societal pressure that compels a particular gender to behave in a particular sexual manner that distinguishes between being masculine or feminine. The story is a perfect example of the multi-marginalisation of a woman like Bindu.

Mrinal and Bindu share a close bond in the house as the former is extremely beautiful and the latter being the ugliest (as both get neglected because of their appearances). Bindu becomes a gateway (as made her realise her own worth) to the independent activist Mrinal, which leads her to ultimate freedom, both physically and mentally. The pathos of Bindu's life is depicted as she is labelled as 'ill-fated' and hence she prefers Death over Marriage. In this society, a woman's life is meant to serve man at any cost. Bindu's sister says; "Bindi, you know that a husband is the sole end of a woman's life. If you are fated to suffer, no one can divert it" (213). At Mrinal's house she cannot stay and at other place, she does not want to, so, she commits suicide. There is no space for the life of Bindu anywhere and she is so unwanted that she starts feeling self-dejection. Tagore's story questions the patriarchal norms where a woman is forced to kill herself, why not man. Through the character portrayal of Mrinal, Tagore opines his ideas about equality, need of freedom, access to education. "This is all play-acting. That may be so, but one should reflect why this play-acting takes its toll only of the saris of Bengali women, not of the dhotis of the brave Bengali gentlemen" (217). Mrinal, at last, decides to resist against these stereotyped ideologies and shatters all ties with her husband and family. This story is a beautiful depiction of evolution of a character from being submissive to aggressive.

These chosen short-stories help in showing that in the era where patriarchy played a significant role in restricting women's freedom, Tagore took up the matter and wrote for the freedom of women in a male-oriented society. Mrinal took all the masculine attributes and tried to defend Bindu from any kind of oppression and subjugation.

Conclusion

In a society, there are attributes that have been assigned to a particular gender, and they must abide by those attributes only. If any of the genders dares to adopt the opposite one, then society starts questioning about their identity and gender. But in the modern world, no one is forced or compelled to act in a particular manner, instead, does whatever pleases him/her. A woman takes the responsibilities of a man and exhibits masculine characteristics despite the fact that she will be judged by a certain number of people who claim to be proponents of power hegemony. But people have become well civilised and understand the need for equal involvement of women in society's construction. Another thing which can be put forth is that why are women always looked as inferior or weak, even men can go through the same thing if they do not possess masculinity. In a patriarchal culture, boys and men are also subjected to stereotyping. Men are discouraged from being emotional, gentle, and caring, as well as from admitting weakness or fear. As in the case of Pyarimohan (Uma's husband), he feels bad for his wife and cares for her, but could not show his concern publicly as neither society nor his family would accept these feminine aspects. They are forced to be breadwinners, guardians, and warriors. So, it's important to pay close attention to what masculinity does to boys and men. Kamla Bhasin in her essay "Exploring Masculinity" gives insight into gender-roles and how gender operates at different levels; 1) 'level of subjective identity' deals with the idea of our understanding, what we learn, what it means to be a man or woman in a particular society, 2) 'level of institutional practice' teaches about all the assigned attributes for girls and boys, as girls learning domestic science and boys learning maths, 3) 'level of ideologies and doctrines' is all about religion, systems of thought, and political doctrines and their assumptions about women and men, femininity and masculinity, and finally, 4) 'symbolic level' where certain signs and symbols are used to depict specific sex and gender, to denote all kinds of norms, qualities, virtues, and vices, such as phallus for male power, emotional for women.

These several old traditions are not relevant in today's society where men and women are equal and equally important for the smooth working of a society. And there is no compulsion to act in a certain manner as the situations have changed now and people are equally contributing to the flow of this community. Working women handle work environments and housework flawlessly, and they still prioritise family, managing both at home and at work.

Works Cited

Tagore, Rabindranath. "The Wife's Letter". *Tagore: Short Stories.* Published by Maple Press. 2012.

.... "The Notebook". *Setu.* Accessed on 25 May, 2022.

https://www.seumag.com/2016/11/the-notebook-rabindranath-tagore.html?m=1

Nash, Joy. "Gender Roles in Modern Society". *One World Education.* Accessed on 7 June, 2022.

https://www.oneworldeducation.org/our-students-writing/gender-roles-in-modern-society/

Bhasin, Kamla. "Exploring Masculinity". Accessed on 9 May, 2022.

http://www.womenutc.com/kamla-bhasin-exploring-masculinity/

Beauvoir, Simone De. *The Second Sex*. Published by Vintage Books, London. 2009. Print.

CHAPTER 2

Mothers and Daughters: A Picture of the Immigrant Women Identity in post-Partition Bengal through the study of two characters in Ritwik Ghatak's Film

Bhairab Barman

Historical Backdrop

Bengal stank of the blood of men, women, and children who had died in the carnage of the communal riots at the stroke of midnight on August 15, 1947, as India awoke to life and freedom. The thrill of freedom had been greatly outweighed by the anguish of partition. For those who had lost their families, who had been uprooted from their home – their native ancestral land that connected them spiritually to their forefathers – and who had arrived in Calcutta from what was then East Pakistan (and would later become Bangladesh in 1971) without anything, only to be forced into outlying, impoverished settlements to continue a life of constant struggle and misery, haunted and hounded by traumatising memories – this freedom was a mirage.

It is fair enough to say that 1947 will go down in South Asian history as a year of great significance. The British Parliament's The Independence of India Bill, which was created on July 18th and introduced on July 4th, 1947, provided for the division of the subcontinent into two independent states. India and Pakistan, both observed their independence days on August 15, 1947, and August 14, 1947, respectively. With it, British India's more than 200-year reign over the continent came to an end and the sun set on its era. Mushirul Hassan correctly quoted by Gita Vishwanath and Salma

Malik in their discussion of two concurrent events that shaped the history of the subcontinent – "No other country in the twentieth century has seen two such contrary movements taking place at the same time. If one was popular nationalist movement..., the other was the counter movement of Partition, marked by violence, cruelty, bloodshed, displacement, and massacres" (Yagnik).

In *Remembering Partition: Violence, Nationalism, and History* (2001), Beerendra Pandey urged the requirement to situate the unprecedented historical disaster of the Partition in dialogue with the mundane if not, it would be perceived as "madness" – a large blip that attests to the everyday political environment. This creates catastrophic incomprehension and eliminates any chance for rigorous investigation into the structural flaws, by doing so, it is advantageously pushed outside the scope of the nation's liberal discourse. In a similar vein, it is crucial to reframe women's issues as an ongoing negotiation between, to demonstrate how the extraordinary has been impacted by both ordinary local and extraordinary historical disasters. The brutality of the Partition is a continuation of the nation's historical daily life.

Introduction

In India, partition stories have always entered the public consciousness, more so through film depictions than through already published literary and written works. It claims that the majority of film depictions are based on or have been adapted from some of the best works of Partition literature, including works by Amrita Pritam, Sadat Hasan Manto, Bhishma Sahani, Bapsi Sidhwa, and others. The topic of the partition has long piqued the interest of Indian filmmakers, who have attempted to depict the terrible events in their own cinematic interpretation. The majority of depictions of the partition show the brutal and eerie recollection of violence toward the minority gender, namely women.

Famous Bengali filmmakers like Ritwik Ghatak, Satyajit Ray, and Mrinal Sen, realistically attacked the patriarchal consciousness of the Bengali middle class and made an effort to assess the condition of women in light of the current socio-economic and political environment. However, Ritwik Ghatak was the first Indian filmmaker to add a different dimension to the battle for survival of Bengali refugee women in the context of social restraints and patriarchal rule in post-Partition Bengal. Shoma Chatterjee says,

> Ritwik's women are eternal, infinite, because they are drawn from mythology, interwoven with Marxist ideology and imbued with a Marxist critique of the materialist, immoral, petty bourgeoisie that defined Calcutta when he stepped into it from Bangladesh, where his roots went too deep. In this sense, his female characters are unique and Indian and also have within them the grains of the Universal Woman by virtue of the fact that they are eternal (Chatterji 60).

In an interview even Ritwik Ghatak said,

> The partition of Bengal convulsed our socio-economic and political life. I could not accept the partition of Bengal nor can I accept it today. I have wanted to say as much in those three films. Despite my protestations, '*Meghe Dhaka Tara*', '*Komal Gandhar*', and '*Subarnarekha*' have become a trilogy. Reflect well and you will find the origin of today's problems in the partition. They divided the country and played ducks and drakes with its people (Ghatak).

Ghatak's films mostly deal with the migration of people due to the 1947 Partition and the devastation it caused. He was deeply disturbed and lacerated by the rootless existence of the migrated people, which, in fact, gets depicted in *'Meghe Dhaka Tara'* (1960), *'Komal Gandhar'* (1961) and *'Subarnarekha'* (1965), earning the epithet of the *Partition trilogy* (Ghatak). In the trilogy, he addresses the psychological, personal, and social challenges of the people displaced in the context of the intricate political upheavals that followed their exodus. East Bengal was Ritwik's birthplace. Abandoning one's home and roots and the repercussions thereof left an indelible mark on his creations. He frequently explored the depths of an alienated existence in his films, highlighting his core conception of society. Ghatak was the artist who explored the socioeconomic and political effects of Bengal's partition in his works.

Women in society are basically of two categories: mothers and daughters. If one studies the position of these two categories, he is close to the picture of the whole society including males. Ideologically a Marxist Ritwik Ghatak never failed to situate his characters in contemporary socio-economic scenario. The two characters of the film *Meghe Dhaka Tara* are no exception. If we carefully analyse these two characters, the full picture of women in partition stricken Indian society is before us. It was indeed a bitter struggle for survival, which can be imagined and understood through the character-analysis of the film.

Nita as a Representative of the Daughters of the Migrants

One can find Ghatak's films, which pragmatistically positioned women's concerns inside a praxis of everyday violence, precisely within the theoretical underpinnings. The burden of the 19th century gendered cultural nationalism that imagined the Nation/Bengal as the great nurturing Mother had made women's bodies into loaded spaces where nation building was to be negotiated. This is why Nita and Sita's tragedies are not unique in time or geography. Up until Partition and the time after, its ubiquitous and twisted effects persisted throughout the Nationalist movement. The refugee women's new positions as advocates and providers have been praised for allowing them to assert their presence in the more public environment, which was once overwhelmingly male-dominated.

The literary source of Ghatak's *Meghe Dhaka Tara* is Bengali writer Shaktipada Rajguru's story *Chenamukh*. The struggle of a Bengali working class woman, Nita, in a suburban colony of Calcutta, finds full expression in the film. It, in fact, turns into a very important document of the great migration due to the Partition. Ghatak turns his film – through the depiction of Nita's character into a phenomenon of a post-migration society. The cruel indifferences of family members towards Nita who sacrifices everything for her family a complex dimension of the position of women in the then society. Kumari Sahani rightly commented:

> The breaking up of society is visualised as a three-way division of womanhood. The three principal woman characters embody the traditional aspects of feminine power. The heroine, Nita, has the preserving and nurturing quality; her sister, Gita, is the sensual woman; their mother represents the cruel aspects. (Sahani 166)

The cause of Nita's tragedy is her inability to blend all three traits, choosing instead to focus solely on the nurturing trait. If Nita's exploitation is the emphasis of *Meghe Dhaka Tara*, then Ghatak's identification of Nita with Jagaddhatri – the Mother Goddess who sustains the universe – conveys a wealth of complexity. The terms 'Jagat' and 'dharan' both refer to the universe. Ghatak symbolically represents the Mother Goddess' role that is placed on and internalised by Nita because the day of her birth coincides with the day of 'Jagaddhatri Puja'. Her family and she accept the job without hesitation, but there is no sign of the respect that a goddess would ordinarily inspire – the term "devi" has been debased to "dasi" in the process. Nita's disease, notably her TB, which is shown as a metaphor, is used by Ghatak to criticise mythology as a tool of torture. The 'devi-dasi' duality itself, mirrored in Nita's compliance in her slavery in an atmosphere of divinity, ultimately consumes her.

In *Meghe Dhaka Tara*, Nita's persona is fully representative. She fights not just to provide for her family despite severe socioeconomic hardships, but also to keep the family together in the face of a raging economic catastrophe. Her strong sense of compassion and desire to uphold intra-familial, unselfish connections are the roots. When defining Nita's personality, Ghatak placed particular emphasis on two facets. He emphasised the portrayal of a lady making sacrifices for her family's financial stability, which serves as a remark on the socioeconomic hardships experienced by a family that has been uprooted from its home in a colony. Second, Nita's helplessness highlights then social norms, or more specifically, the dominant patriarchal mindset. It needs to be emphasised that the ladies of the refugee families did not suddenly leave their homes to find work because they believed in women's independence or freedom. The reality was different. The uprooted families removed the conventional social restraints on their womenfolk and allowed them to go out and earn a living due to the crushing poverty. The only reason the uprooted families created this small haven of freedom for women was to provide for them safety and comfort. Ghatak contrasted the sacrifice made by a young woman for her family with the family's exploitation and deprivation of her – or, to put it another way, by society. A refugee family's rehabilitation came at the expense of life, and life was sacrificed on the altar of death. Following the partition of Bengal, many of immigrant women struggled to make a living. Nita's struggle for life – her dreams, her dashed dreams, and her death – become a metaphor for their struggles.

Nita's Mother as a Representative of the Migrant Mothers

The mother of Nita is a typical East Bengali refugee housewife who is torn apart by the daily hard fight for survival and is driven to measure all relationships in terms of generating income. She chastises her eldest son as a result, which makes him decide to leave the house. She makes it quite plain to her eldest son that if one cannot work, one forfeits the opportunity to eat meals at home. She finds Nita's friendship with Sanat disturbing. She worries that if Nita weds Sanat, the family would no longer have a means of support. Her eldest son, Sankar, leaves home to pursue a career as an artist, Gita to pursue a happy marriage, and Mantu to advance in society. Nita's mother doesn't seem too concerned about anything. She clings on Nita like a spider since she is the only source of support and the family's only chance at survival. Unknowingly, she allows Nita to become into a tool for making money. Nita is worried when her father brings up the subject of her marriage since she knows that would be disastrous for the family.

If skillfully analysed, the character of Nitas's mother is firmly rooted in reality. In this perspective, it is also important to note that, despite the excessive symbolism Ghatak gives some of his female characters, some of them are very much of this world, full of flesh and blood. In *Meghe Dhaka Tara*, Nita's mother embodies this type of character who feels it is her responsibility as a housewife to ensure the survival of her family, which includes her sons and daughters. The issue of morality and purity is unimportant in this survival need. She so desires Nita, her earning daughter, to live a maiden life. She is unable to put her faith in Nita's selfless act. She is driven to selfishness and mistrust of her daughter Nita by her paralysing fear of her family's financial downfall. Problematic is Nita's mother's personality, though. Ghatak did neither represent her as a horrible stereotyped greedy woman nor as a symbol of selflessness because he was fully aware of the difficulties a housewife in a refugee family experienced. Faced with tremendous poverty, she feels in danger; but, she also feels compelled to safeguard and preserve it despite the difficulties.

Ritwik contrasted the suffering that comes with losing a loved one to partition and migration. He focused on the psychological aspect of the issue of women rather than limiting himself to the issue of the displaced people as that of the division of a geographical entity. Ritwik's works surely acquired a distinctive personality via the depiction of the alienation and mental suffering endured by the uprooted women. He had no desire to analyse the partition issue in its most obvious form. Instead, he focused on how these women despite living in great poverty, lost sight of human values and abandoned social objectives in favour of survival.

Conclusion

Nita is the symbol of all suffering women of the migration due to the Partition. She is a representative of the striving self-sufficient Bengali women of the then contemporary society. Later on, empowered women line her was a common phenomenon. They even were starting to take part in politics and decision making affairs as well. They suffered immensely due to the Partition but ultimately they got strengthened in the post-Independence era. The post-migration women broke the taboos of the traditional society and started emerging in the job market. Slowly the non-refugee women were also influenced by the working class refugee women. The Bengali women seemed no longer the showpieces of private life and child-bearing domesticities. Patriarchal controls were getting flexible to a vast extent. And, they were getting represented in fictions and films.

Undoubtedly, the refugee women opened the way for subsequent generations of Bengali working women and activists, especially within the Left politics. However, to equate this coming out with emancipation and the exercise of agency reduces the issue to a panegyric. The interstices of the daily, routine violence that the immigrant women had to contend with and how they had seen their own actions are lost when we examine the process through the prisms of trauma. *Meghe Dhaka Tara* by Ghatak has some of the most delicate, practical, and sympathetic depictions of refugee women's sufferings in the dystopian post-Partition society.

A thousand voices of a thousand refugee women, now lost in oblivion, yet they return to us like odour-remnants of the last embers of a long-gone era, shall always haunt us in Nita's desperate and anguished affirmation of life as she grabs onto her brother Shankar in the penultimate scene as she is slowly moving towards her imminent death at the sanatorium. The Shillong hills are still filled with the sound of her cries of thousands of migrant women:

"*Dada, ami baachte chaai* (Dada, I want to live!)"

Works Cited

Chatterji, Shoma. A. *Ritwik Ghatak: The Celluloid Rebel.* New Delhi: Rupa & Co., 2004. Print.

Ghatak, Ritwik. "Ritwik on Ritwik: An Interview." *Chitrabikshan* (1975): 57-58.

Pandey, Beerendra. "Remembering Partition: Violence, Nationalism and History in India" *Intellectual Discourse* 9.2 (2001).

Ritwik, Ghatak. "Rows and rows of fences." (2000).

Sahani, Kumar. Ajantrik. Ed. Dipankar Bhattacharya. *Hooghly: Uttarpara Cine Club*, 2000. Print.

Yagnik, P. R. (2013). *The Partition in Fictional and Film Version: A Critical Study of the Novels and the Films based on Partition.* Retrieved October 2018, from Shodhganga: http://hdl.handle.net/10603/46058

CHAPTER 3

Denying the Popular Notion of Femininity: A Comparative Study of Gender Role in the Chitrangada Myth

Manidip Chakraborty

Abstract

Popular Indian modes of entertainment, chiefly Indian films, have always celebrated the victory of the beautiful feminine heroine. However, the trope of femininity, a construction of the male gaze, has always been a delimiting factor for the true identity of the female. Like Tagore's heroine Chitrangada, all these powerful women from the East and the West alike must put on the garb of feminine identity in order to qualify as acceptable heroines. This act of self-denial has been highlighted and problematised in many texts and movies in the past. It is only through the proper understanding as well as acceptance of one's true identity that a heroine can truly liberate herself from the binding forces of art and life.

Keywords: Feminine, identity, self, role, denial, acceptance, transformation

Introduction

In popular Hindi cinema of the last few decades, it is almost customary for the heroine to exhibit all the necessary feminine charms in order to qualify as the desirable woman of the dream. In Baahubali: The Beginning (2015), for example, there is this heroine, Avantika, who doesn't seem to care about feminine virtues because she has much more pressing problems in life. It is however, the hero's erotic dream which sees in her a beautiful woman possessing all the defining feminine aspects, and she must change her real face to fit into the mask (literally). This is followed by a battle of sex, which is very important to the heroine even though it is just fun for the hero. The battle is over when the hero vanishes and leaves behind the stunned heroine, visibly dazzled by the reflection of the beautiful woman the hero has turned her into. The real problem now begins, as the newly awakened awareness of her own feminine virtues has only made her weaker, and in the moments that follow, she does not appear to be the same warrior whose amazing combat skills had earlier impressed the hero and the viewer's alike.

Avantika now needs to be protected by the hero at every step. Now she cannot be trusted anymore to continue her assigned task, that is, freeing the captive queen Devasena. Ironically enough, her transformation from the "female" (a biological truth) to the "feminine" (a social construction, or rather an ideological abstraction) is the reason another woman remains in the chain (Showalter 32). Perhaps Devasena is not the only woman whose freedom remains far from being attained due to the phallocentric doctrines successfully infecting women like Avantika. The moment Avantika stops challenging her male counterparts in terms of possessing physical prowess and battle skills (traditionally known as male domains), she is no more a threat to the male gaze. Now she becomes relegated to the background, merely an insignificant character throughout the rest of the story, and her psychological and emotional recesses are never explored any further. In order to highlight the heroism of the male protagonist then, as always, the 'manly' features of a very powerful female character had to be toned down, if not utterly sacrificed. Of course, Baahubali could be read as a multilayered text that purposefully brings these sexual politics to the forefront before leaving them unresolved. After all, it's a popular, somewhat escapist movie that doesn't seem to have a clear goal for its audience.

The very idea that the heroine of a romance must be a damsel in distress, one who perennially needs the protection and guidance of the masculine hero, is however no invention of the 20th or 21st century popular Hindi cinema. The debate surrounding this kind of gender-based discrimination has been there even in the *Mahabharata*, in the mythical story of Chitrangada, the fabled warrior princess of Manipur, who would eventually become one of the wives of Arjuna, perhaps the greatest male warrior of the time. In Rabindranath Tagore's 1892 dance-drama *Chitrangada,* the moral and psychological dilemma of the titular princess has been explored at great length, with a considerable emphasis on the importance of possessing or not possessing the determining garb known as femininity. She has been raised like a prince and trained in all the skills (warfare, archery, polity and politics) necessary to qualify as a warrior prince. Perhaps at once stage this rigorous training has been a denial of her gender, her true identity, but right now it has made her who she is, and she would not change this self for anything not worth it. For Arjuna, at least in the beginning of the play, the princess, in her imitation of the image of a male warrior, is nothing more than a 'joke' ('*koutuka*' in Bengali). Arjuna does make an important point here – Chitrangada desperately presenting herself in 'manly' attire is an act of self-mockery, or rather self-denial. But then, Arjuna is no advocate of gender equality, and he seems only interested in reminding Chitrangada of the gender-specific roles she must conform to. The *kshatriya dharma* seems to be the monopoly of the male prince only, and any violation of the rules regarding *varna* (remember Ekalavya or Karna) or gender would be severely punished by the law-makers of society.

There is only one way for Chitrangada to be accepted by Arjuna's code of chivalry – Chitrangada must not venture into the male territory, and she must instead try to make herself more attractive or in other words, more 'feminine'. And this is what prepares the premise for Chitrangada to transform herself into '*Surupa*' (that is, the beautiful) and get immediately accepted by Arjuna, who seems enamoured of her womanly charm. Reminding one of Keats' *Lamia* though, the irony of the situation lies in the interplay of appearance and reality; Arjuna has only fallen in love with what she is not, and not what she actually is. Here, the shadow is more important than the substance itself. In Keats' poem however, Lycius, the lover, knows the actual identity of Lamia, the serpent woman. When the sage Apollonius makes his disciple face the naked truth, the castle of illusion false apart, Lamia comes back to her 'ugly' self, and Lycius dies immediately. It is debatable whether the ugly truth was really more desirable than the beautiful falsehood, which at least sustained the two lovers. Now in Tagore's treatment of the myth of Chitrangada, there is no Apollonius to bring the truth to the surface, and the heroine successfully plays along the criteria needed to be fulfilled for her acceptance. She might not represent the truth in this case, but she becomes beauty personified in the determining gaze of Arjuna, and that is really important for her.

So in a way, it is the male fantasy of wanting the desirable woman to appear in a very specific manner that determines her appearance. This should remind one of Alfred Hitchcock's movie *Vertigo*, in which the hero makes a woman undergo rigorous outward changes to meet the notion of the desirable woman in his mind. When stripped of all its suspense and thriller elements, the story considers how a forceful transformation might lead to the 'killing' (here literally though) of the true identity of the woman. The prospect of the hero both making and marring the heroine makes it clear that the woman is not more than a toy-like existence in the clutches of the hero.

Chitrangada has thus made a compromise to conform to the norms of male acceptance. But this act of self-denial only complicates the gender related issues in the play. It was Arjuna who once dressed himself up as a woman during his hiatus (or, *agyatvas*) in the Virata city. That was merely a disguise meant to hide his (gender?) identity. But the predicament of Chitrangada is just the opposite – even though she is in the guise of a man, this is what she really is, and not merely a false impression. The moment she starts presenting herself as a feminine figure, that is when she starts donning a disguise. This should immediately bring to mind the Shakespearean heroines such as Viola (*Twelfth Night*), Rosalind (*As You Like It*) and Portia (*The Merchant of Venice*), who all put on male disguises at different stages of these plays to gain access to the abundant 'male' authority for serving their separate purposes. The one important aspect that binds these three plays together is the fact that, as per the trajectory of romantic comedies, theses heroine must not remain forever in the male domain of authority, and they must come back to the 'normal' world and accept their compartmentalised, gender-oriented, feminine roles by the end of the play. The reward is almost always acceptance into some kind of institutionalised domestic bliss – each of these plays concludes with the beautiful heroine marrying the charming hero. But what she loses in the bargain is the momentary taste of freedom – as the feminine heroine of a romance she cannot claim the authority she once exerted as a woman in the guise of a man.

On the flip side of the coin, there is also the tragic predicament of Lady Macbeth in Shakespeare's *Macbeth*, who also invaded successfully into the male domain of ambition, crime and violence. But unlike the heroines of the romantic comedies, Lady Macbeth has to pay for her non-sanctioned journey into the male discourse, as well as for her willing denial of her feminine self. She is cursed with loneliness, rendered insane and it is assumed she has to commit suicide to atone for her engulfing sense of guilt. With the switching of the trajectory from comic to tragic, therefore, the severity of the punishment also changes considerably.

Compared to the three heroines of the Shakespearean romantic comedies, Chitrangada's transformation happens a bit too early in the play, perhaps because Tagore is intending to turn the accepted trajectory of a Shakespearean romantic comedy upside down and engage in a far more theoretical debate on accepted gender roles. Also, her disguise has always been the imposed feminine self and not the 'manly' appearance which she has now integrated into her very self and made it her reality. For her then the coming back to what is 'normal' is just the opposite of the Shakespearean heroines – she must reject the masquerade of femininity before the play ends. Also she must be accepted as what she is if the ending has to be counted as somewhat 'happy'. Tagore's story is also bearing the basic framework of a Romance, although it is not primarily concerned with providing entertainment and fun to the audience in the way a Shakespearean comedy usually does. The very fact that Chitrangada does successfully play any gender role as per the demand of the situation is what makes her stand apart from a Rosalind or a Viola who seems always uncomfortable with her disguise. This element of fluidity further complicates the question of gender roles; is it possible, or even necessary, to transform oneself as per the requirement of the male discourse? This only highlights how ephemeral this transformation must be.

In G.B. Shaw's drama *Pygmalion*, it is through acquiring the magical power of language and social mannerism that the heroine Eliza transforms herself into a duchess-like figure that would be accepted by the upper class of late Victorian British society. One important aspect of this process of transformation is that the decision is entirely Eliza's own, even though it is the Midas touch of Professor Henry Higgins, the phonetician, which later on turns the piece of stone into a living being. Similarly, Chitrangada, re-enacting the myths of the ugly duckling or Cinderella alike, out of no compulsion perhaps, decides to undergo a series of transformations in her outlook. The question of knowledge and ignorance is of the utmost importance here. Chitrangada is conscious of her false enactment of womanhood, whereas for Arjuna it is something normal, something representing the Truth. This also indicates how a set of externally imposed codes can be truer than truth itself. The acceptance of this falsehood by the male gaze only institutionalises the whole thing as normative. Arjuna is not just ignorant of Chitrangada's reality, he simply does not care. Unless she meets the necessary qualities, she simply fails to get 'sold' to the prince charming. The mercantile language is intended to underscore how the heroine must present herself as a saleable commodity in a society that has always been consumerist.

The transformation from *Kurupa* (the ugly one) to *Surupa* (the beautiful one) is necessitated by the intervention of Madan, the god of love. This runs parallel to the Greek myth of Pygmalion in which Galatea becomes a beautiful lady due to the magic of goddess Venus/Aphrodite. In each case, as one feels, there is a perceived infringement of the laws of nature. For Pygmalion the sculptor, the very act of falling in love with his own creation Galatea is no less than an act of incest; a social taboo since the birth of civilisation. Similarly the myth of Chitrangada shows how the happy conjugal life she gets to spend with Arjuna for the tenure of one year is a very elaborate fabrication conceived by the conspiracy of Madan and Vasanta, the two gods having full sway over human passion and emotion. Once again, the absence of reason (in *Lamia* it was the absence of Apollonius) is what makes the entire affair unnatural, somewhat ethically wrong. Moreover, Arjuna has remained a celibate for past twelve years and is supposed to continue to be so for a couple of years more until his tenure of *brahmacharya* comes to an end. Finally, Chitrangada enticing Arjuna by appearing as what she is not is ultimately an act of deception, of betrayal. It is therefore not wrong to consider their union as not something natural, and it is most likely to fall apart after the trance is once over.

Finally, the Chitrangada myth seems to hinge on the question of being absolutely honest to oneself and to one's partner alike. The span of one year is also a reminder that the trance created by a false impression is bound to be dated, and the truth is the ultimate beauty (almost an echo of the Keatsean dictum) that should prevail irrespective of its inherent flaws. Is this span of one year also a reference to the seasonal cycle, which defeats the spell cast by the gods of love and intoxication? In that case, nature stands victorious over the artificial, the concocted. The false paradise (Is this what Jean Baudrillard would call 'hyperreality'?) created by Madan and Vasanta is bound to give way to the more mundane and less dramatic reality. The trance is finally over and, following the trajectory of a traditional romance, Chitrangada comes clean before Arjuna, who in turn accepts her with her 'imperfect' beauty. Unlike Shakespeare's Romantic Comedies and Hindi movies like Kuch Kuch Hota Hai

(1998), Tanu Weds Manu (2011), Hasee Toh Phasee (2014), and of course Baahubali, Tagore's play goes from ugly to beautiful and then back to ugly, but it ends on a happy note.

Considering the common trajectory of traditional romances, therefore, Tagore's ending might even appear to the reader/audience as anticlimactic, or even lacking enough entertaining value. Tagore's play, however, conveys a very important message that is strikingly absent in much of the popular art forms seemingly obsessed with the feminine virtues as the ultimate gateway to the heroine's success in winning the trophy of an eligible partner. Even Chitrangada follows this same path for a while (for a year, to be precise), but then seems to come to terms with the real definition of beauty, before it is too late. On a final note, Tagore's heroine might be considered alongside Eliza, the heroine of Shaw's play. Just like many other transformed heroines, Eliza does remain the beautiful woman she has presently become. But she is now in full control of her own life, and she can choose virtually everything for herself – her profession, her life partner, etc. The proper internalisation of all these acquired traits has made sure that she does not appear as a fake personality. Similarly, the real 'happy' thing about Chitrangada's fate is that she did not have to transform herself for getting accepted by the best partner around (which reminds one of G.B. Shaw's philosophy of Life Force). She is thus spared the artificial fate that most of the romantic heroines have traditionally been subjected to.

Works Cited

Keats, John. *Lamia, Isabella, The Eve of St. Agnes, and Other Poems*, 1820. Otley, West Yorkshire; Washington, D.C.: Woodstock Books, 2001. Print.

Shakespeare, William. *The Oxford Shakespeare: The Complete Works of William Shakespeare*. London ; New York: H. Milford, Oxford University Press, 1924. Print.

Shaw, George Bernard. Pygmalion. Dover Publications, 1994. Print.

Showalter, Elaine. *A Literature of Their Own: British Women Novelists from Bronte to Lessing*. Princeton, N.J: Princeton University Press, 1999. Print.

Smith, John D. *The Mahabharata*. London: Penguin, 2009. Print.

Tagore, Rabindranath. *Collected Poems and Plays of Rabindranath Tagore*. New York, Macmillan Co. 1949. Print.

CHAPTER 4

Reconnoitering Caste and Gender Inequity in Baburao Bagul's *When I Hid My Caste*

Dr. Kailash Kumar

Abstract

Indian Dalit literature truly represents the Indian Dalits as the despicable and homeless. In doing so, the intention of the Indian Dalit writers is to resist the conservative policy of living and writing which both upper caste Hindus and canonical writers forced on the lower castes and outcastes (Dalits) in Indian society. In my present exposition, I shall make a modest effort to espouse how Indian Dalit literature writers especially Baburao Bagul (1931-2008) in his collection of stories entitled *When I Hid My Caste* (2018) present a porthole to look at the misuse of power by the upper caste Hindus. I shall also focus upon the general inclination of Indian Dalit literature with special reference to Bagul's stories. The present paper shall try to endorse how Indian Dalit literature in general and Baburao Bagul's stories in particular, carves the life of the Dalits as the despicable and homeless in the context of caste-filled Indian society. I shall analyse the predominant theme of caste and gender discrimination in *When I Hid My Caste* through the lens of Dalit feminism. All the ten stories in *When I Hid My Caste*, are full of atrocities and discrimination in the form of murder, lynching, social ostracisation, economic exploitation, and sexual abuse against the Dalits particularly Dalit women. A Dalit woman is doubly suppressed, first for being a Dalit and secondly for being a woman. Moreover, she is placed at the ending of the hierarchy of women.

Keywords: caste, Dalit, gender, revolt, self-assertion, women

Introduction

When I Hid My Caste is a Dalit text written by a Dalit writer that takes into account the trauma, pain, resistance and protest related to a major segment of the population i.e. the Dalits (outcastes). In the opening story titled *Prisoner of Darkness*, the protagonist being a Dalit woman, is forced to undergo pain and suffering by the upper caste people. The suffering results in revolt by the woman's son against those sitting at the top echelons of power. In *Bohada*, there is a strong note of dissent as the central character Dammu raises his head in self-assertion against the powerful members of the village. The physical power of the protagonist of *Gangster* is compatible to that of a bull or tiger even though the core human values are still alive in his heart. In *Dassehra Sacrifice*, the Dalit characters shine throughout the ritual of Dassehra sacrifice as against the upper class members of the village. The protagonist of *Monkey*, beats and thrashes his wife after a lower caste member defeats him in the wrestling match. In *Streetwalker*, Girija is such a woman who is compelled to walk on the streets and is sexually exploited as she does not have enough money to visit her ailing son in the village. In the story *Competition*, the female protagonist wins the sympathy of the readers when she behaves like a prostitute in order to earn money to save her ailing husband. Thus, Baburao Bagul's stories spark revolt and protest and not just misery and despair. The stories breathe fresh life in the arena of Dalit literature. Bama says, "The primary motive of Dalit literature is the liberation of Dalits in particular and the liberation of the oppressed in general." (Bama, 1999, p.97)

The story *Prisoner of Darkness* depicts the imprisonment of a Dalit woman by the upper caste men. Banoo is the daughter of an untouchable. Many men tried to buy her with the intention of satiating their lust. Her father did not want her to become the wife of ten different men. Neither did he want her to go to a brothel. Therefore, Banoo, the lower caste woman, is bought by Ramrao Deshmukh with the promise that she would be his beloved only and nobody else's. Ramrao Deshmukh, an extremely wealthy man, also happened to be the chief of the village. Ramrao was old enough to be Banoo's father in age. In order to avoid his anger and to prevent him from turning her out of his house, she obeyed all his orders. She even paid no attention to her baby Daulat. After the birth of her son Daulat she did not give birth to any other child as "in order to prevent other babies from coming along, she had her tubes tied on Ramrao's orders." (Bagul: 18). She even sacrificed her maternal love as she subjected her son to the wicked environment of the 'wada' (traditional Maharashtrian home) and the tradition of village. Since childhood Daulat was left to bear the brunt of the entire village as he was criticised by everybody which drove him mad. The insults had distorted his mind. The disdain had made him tight lipped. An indistinct personality had been imprinted in his mind due to the disgrace forced upon him by the advantaged upper-caste people. The story describes his split personality as he is born out of an unlawful sexual relationship between an upper-caste wealthy landowner father and a Dalit woman. He had to bear this insult for such a long time that it had turned him into a violent person. When he asked for water to drink from an upper caste woman, she refused to do so as she says, "I'll give up my life but I won't give you water." (Bagul: 13). Another man started levelling charges against his mother: "That prostitute has ruined everything. Tomorrow every Mang, Mahar and Chamar is going to turn up at a Brahmin's house and ask for water. The whore has soiled all notions of caste and creed". (Bagul: 13). Banoo knew all this about her son and "she writhed in torment on his behalf." (Bagul: 18).

The Indian society has been split up into four major castes namely, Brahmin, Kshatriya, Vaishya, and Shudra. A Sudra stands at the lowest stratum of the Indian society and is commonly known as dalit or untouchable. In all aspects of life, the Dalits or the untouchables are the one who are suppressed, shamed, subjugated, prejudiced and marginalised. The term 'Dalit' refers to the oppressed, broken and downtrodden. Dalit literature has got a long past. In spite of a long history, Dalit storybooks were not given due recognition mainly because the literary output was controlled by the chosen few. Dalit literature started coming out when the Dalits appeared as a dominant group in the political arena. Dr. B. R. Ambedkar's Dalit movement of 1927 was, "the enabling factor in Dalit literature because of his ideas, outlook towards life and his struggle to achieve what he felt just" (Dangle: p. xxiii).

Prisoner of Darkness deals with the multiple themes of gender prejudice, sexual abuse, social intolerance, exploitation of dalits and caste inequity. Banoo, the protagonist of the story sacrificed her own life as well as the life of her son in order to make her husband Ramrao happy. Instead of sympathising with her, the upper caste people looked at her with disdain as the author says, "They should have sympathised with her and held Ramrao accountable; instead, the hidebound village felt only contempt for her;" (Bagul: 19). When Ramrao died, his son Devaram held Banoo responsible for his father's death. He did not recognise Banoo as the rightful wife of his father as she was an untouchable. He did not regard her as his mother as he says, "I am a Deshmukh. I am not the son of some streetwalker, some shameless low-caste woman. Prostitutes don't have sons; they only have bastards." (Bagul: 15). With an intention to kill and rape his step mother, Devaram ran after Banoo. Banoo started running out of the house and into the street in order to save her life. She asked for help but the upper caste people were only laughing at her miserable condition as an old woman remarks, "Slut, whore, a woman like you has not been born in all the three worlds." (Bagul: 17). Daulat, the son of an untouchable woman, sacrifices his life in order to save his mother's modesty from being destroyed by the upper caste people. The incident is a grim reminder of the class and caste conflict that has been a recurring feature of the age old Indian society. T.S. Eliot says that "each class should have constant additions and defections; the classes while remaining distinct should be able to mix freely." (Eliot: 50).

In *Prisoner of Darkness* the storywriter denounces the sexual exploitation of a dalit woman named, Banoo. Banoo, being a low born woman is a victim of the sexism that existed in the Dalit settlements. Bagul sensibly portrays the sexual exploitation of Dalit women by the high caste men. The story is important as it sincerely portrays the bleak realism of the Dalit world, the example of heartrending humanness, pursuit for distinctive self and Bagul's sympathetic attitude towards women. The author portrays the deep pain of Banoo and his son, Daulat, who have been let down, oppressed and forced to suffer. Daulat is labeled as an 'illegitimate' child. The sufferer swallows the bitter pill of illegitimacy from infancy which is an insult to human self-respect. Daulat senses alienation in his upper-caste father's house He is regarded as a 'bastard' by his step brothers and other members of his father's family. During the early years of his life, he develops awareness about the scheme of untouchability. Here Bagul portrays the vulnerability of the Dalits and their animal-like way of life and also constant struggle in opposition to scarcity and starvation. Several questions arise from the story concerning the pain, anguish and distress of the Dalits that make their lives tragic. Dalit literature attained a separate idiom through its varied nature that defied leading literary standard. Baburao Bagul's *When I Hid My Caste* puts marginalisation, discrimination, isolation and humiliation of the dalits at the forefront. It looks at the tragic condition of dalit women in the Indian social order. Basu observes: "Dalits became victims of their own dalit consciousness which, instead of transcending caste and caste based hierarchies, strengthened as untouchable because of their low caste status." (Basu, 361).

Bagul's narrative depicts the bestial and evils nature of the upper-caste people as well as the patriarchy. It portrays their ruthless behavior with the powerless Dalit women and children. A revolutionary in the form of Daulat is born in the narrative. The narrator recognises the predicament of the untouchables with firmness. Bagul kicks off an uncompromising debate on the longstanding hierarchy of caste system as he explores the caste system with all its evil consequences. He is decisive in his revelation of the cruelty and brutality of the upper-caste.

Baburao Bagul is a staunch dalit feminist. *When I Hid My Caste* relates an account of never-ending despair, brutal persecution and shocking gender bias. A dalit woman experiences two types of marginalisation. First she is marginalised for being a woman and second for belonging to the family of the untouchables. Hence she is "doubly oppressed." In *Prisoner of Darkness*, Banoo is doubly exploited as she is an untouchable woman. Dalit feminism reveals the absence of a gender viewpoint in the Dalit resistance. This type of feminism highlights the fact that in the dalit world, a woman exists under the shadow of both caste and patriarchy. Bama a well-known contemporary dalit feminist writer from Tamil Nadu reveals, "My mind is crowded with many anecdotes: stories not only about the sorrows and tears of dalit women, but also about their lively and rebellious culture, passion about life with vitality, truth, enjoyment and about their hard labour." (Bama, 2005, p.9).

Bagul's story *Streetwalker* describes the plight and tragic death of a woman protagonist, Girja. Girja did not want to walk on the streets and pass time with other man who would sexually offend her in return for some money. Kasaam the owner of a restaurant told her a lie that her son was ill back in the village. Actually her son was already dead. However, the moment Girja came to know that her son was ill, she wanted to go to the village in order to see her ailing son. But she did not have money and therefore, "Girja began to wail and weep. She threw herself at his (Kasaam's) feet, begging him for a loan so she could go to the village." (Bagul: 34). Unable to get help she decided to restart her job of a streetwalker. She was compelled to sleep with a man with the promise that he will pay her a certain amount of money. The man lured her into a hotel and sexually abused her in the night. However when she demanded the money, he thrashed her so badly that she was almost dead. Girja was a mother and so she sacrificed her life for her son: "a mother maddened by love, burned by her own sorrow, she fell and she lay where she had fallen." (Bagul: 39). The male dominated society is no better than a vulture that tore the body and soul of a woman, Girja, into bits and pieces.

Women are made to stand as sex symbol in a patriarchal society. They become victim to sexual pestering and mistreatment. Dalit feminist literature exposes the cruel ill-treatment that a dalit woman goes through in her lifetime. Bagul enriches both the rich tradition of the dalit movement and the women's interest group in India whenever he selects a female as the central character of his narrative. He creates such Dalit women who are daring and courageous with a power to revolt. This he does by discussing daily activities of dalit society. In that sense his stories are totally removed from the traditional narrative. Bama says, "Dalits are the most economically oppressed, culturally ostracised and politically marginalised people in modern India" (Bama, 1999, p. 97).

In the story *Monkey*, a wrestler when defeated by his opponent becomes angry. Bapu Pehelwan gets defeated in the wrestling match by a member of the lower caste. Moreover, the winner belongs to his in-laws' village and therefore Bapu is not able to digest it as the author says, "That it should have been someone of a lower caste and the man should have come from that particular area made it worse." (Bagul: 54). To hide his failure, he curses his wife Sakhu. Bapu and his mother presumed that Sakhu was responsible for his defeat and therefore she was his enemy. He was so enraged by this that he even considered murdering his wife and disposing her off. He took a vow of celibacy in order to defeat his rival but he was at the same time struggling with the demon of lust. Though his mother had strictly prohibited him from coming near his wife, but the moment he saw her "he had her by the hair and was dragging her up to press her against his body." (Bagul: 54). When he realised that he had broken his vow to remain celibate, he was filled with rage. Therefore, he threw his wife Sakhu, away from him. When she fell, "she hit the bamboo shutters with great force. Her nose began to bleed and her lips and face began to swell up." (Bagul: 56). Bapu was so cruel that he was not at all bothered about the bleeding nose and swollen face of his wife. He felt so fearful of his mother and shameful at having broken his vow of celibacy that he became uncontrollably angry. He held his wife responsible for what had happened without holding himself responsible for all the wrongdoings. He began hating her so much that he wanted to see her dead. He wanted to crack her head open as one might break a coconut. He went forward to kill her, "But the sight of the rising slopes of her chest and the slenderness of her waist turned his murderous rage into a cruel lust." (Bagul: 57). His mother too gets angry with her daughter in-law. She holds her responsible for breaking the celibacy of her son and thus ensuring his defeat. To calm down his mother, Bapu Pehelwan started beating his wife and asking her the same question as to why she came near him. But she had no answer to her husband's question as she being a Hindu woman worshipped him blindly. On the other hand, he began to throw Sakhu here and there and as a result "Her body went limp, blood spurted from many places, it covered her everywhere." (Bagul: 58).

When I Hid My Caste looks at the disparity among women due to their caste configuration. It explores the verbal communication of dalit women that is loaded with rich meaning. Bagul opposes all types of subjugation and pain that dalit women undergo. His stories lend an optimistic individuality to dalit women by concentrating on their internal power. Through his women centric narrative, Bagul showcases the heart and soul of dalit women. His purpose is to make a plea for improvement in the existence of dalit women. The transformation encompasses diverse areas such as sex and gender bias, privileges to education etc. Bagul's women are not a hopeless lot. They are capable of handling their lives on their own. M. N. Wankhade writes, "The writing that has come forward to forge friendship and harmony between people and literature is Dalit writing." (Wankhade: 329)

The story *Pesuk* deals with the sacrifices made by a woman named Savitri for her husband, Jaidev, and the cruel treatment she receives from him. Savitri sacrificed herself to give her ineffective husband a son. To make sure that her husband remains happy, she even climbed on the funeral pyre and was turned to ash. However, her husband was such an evil and hypocritical 'zamindar' (landlord) that he failed to see her importance. Jaidev married many times and Savitri was his sixth wife. Polygamy is such an evil practice in the society that it has destroyed the life of many women. Jaidev married for the seventh time and in the process he not only killed his sixth wife Savitri but also her son. A *pesuk* is an evil spirit that is present in the form of a woman. It was presumed that *Pesuk* tried to avenge the cruelty committed by men against women. The pesuk did not kill women but it helped them. On the other hand, it cut the nose of men. However Savitri was not a pesuk. She had the strength and power of Mother Ganga. In truth and beauty she was immortal like the sun. She turned into an awful ghost as her husband tortured her so badly. Her beautiful body had been severely damaged by her cruel husband Jaidev. Her dark hair had become the colour of mud. The beautiful velvety texture of the hair had gone. It was now matted and tangled. There were dark bruises on her rosy forehead. Her head had been labelled and the scar sprinted from her eyebrows to the top of her head. Her straight nose was broken. Her upper lip writhed with anger, like a severed snake's tail. Fury knotted her face and made her ugly. Both her breasts had been cut off. Those people who had cut her left breast had committed an error as small lumps of flesh still lay hanging. Her entire body had been devastated. She mercilessly started attacking people when the evil Jaidev killed her child. The author says: "She was now devoid of humanity, she was like an animal with a bestial cruelty. Like animals, she had a distrust of humans." (Bagul: 89).

Inequality in terms of gender is one of the main social concerns in India. Women suffer frequent aggression and mistreatment in the male-dominated society. The fundamental rights of women especially dalit women are in tatters in our country due to social ill-treatment, sexual harassment and domestic violence. Baburao Bagul is a well-known Dalit author of Maharastra, India. He made people aware of caste and gender discrimination. He seeks to establish a society based on equality. In his stories he talks about ache and anguish of Dalit women as they are doubly marginalised. He highlights the causes of both men and women. Through his collection of stories, Bagul resists against caste, and gender discriminations as M. N. Wankhade writes, "The pens of the Dalit writers are ready as levers to lift the people's democracy out of the mud of anarchy. Because in this mud the Dalits, only the Dalits, have been mired, half-dead, for centuries." (Wankhade: 328).

Conclusion

The Indian society has always been rigid on the issue of caste and gender. The self-declared advantaged groups of people exploit, discriminate and are indifferent, unjust and inhumane towards the so called fragile section of the society. It seems as if the element of humanism has got no presence in the society due to the awful treatment that a person meets from another person of the similar society. Literary writings that discussed the profound suffering of innumerable people based on caste, culture and gender were termed Dalit Literature. These writings made people conscious and therefore helped in controlling the mistreatment of the oppressed people to a great extent: "The untouchables are fighting, and the writing is raising consciousness about human rights among them." (Limbale: 137). Dalit Literature has served as a means to depict the cruel truth of Indian Social structure. It has portrayed the sufferings and anguish of those people who have faced the drudgery for being born in the blighted social structure. It depicts dalits as the powerless sufferers of caste classification and women dalits as doubly subjugated. Baburao Bagul's *When I Hid My Caste* is a Dalit literary text that throws light on the insensitivity of the society towards the abuse of oppressed people by the self-declared honoured category of people. It portrays the resultant resistance against atrocities and discrimination of the patriarchy. That resistance was offered by those people whose lives were trampled but who had resolved to stand up and struggle for their legitimate civil rights.

Works Cited

Bagul, Baburao. *When I Hid My Caste*. Speaking Tiger: New Delhi, 2018.

Bama. "Dalit Literature". Trans. M. Vijayalakshmi. *Indian Literature*, 63(5). Sept.-Oct.,1999, pp. 97-98.

Bama. *Sangati*. trans. Laxmi Holmstrom. New Delhi: OUP, 2005.

Basu, Swaraj. *Readings on Dalit Identity: History, Literature and Religion*. Orient Blackswan, 2016.

Dangle, Arjun. "Introduction". Trans. Avinash S. Pandit and Daya Agrawal. In Arjun Dangle (Ed.), *Poisoned Bread: Translations from Modern Marathi Dalit Literature* (pp. xix-liv). Hyderabad: Orient Blackswan, 2011.

Eliot, T.S. *Notes towards a definition of Culture*. London: Faber, 1962.

Limbale, Sharan Kumar. *Towards an Aesthetic of Dalit Literature: History, Controversies and Considerations*. Trans. Alok Mukherjee. New Delhi: Orient Blackswan, 2004.

Wankhade, M.N, "Friends, the Day of Irresponsible Writers is Over". Trans. Maxine Berntsen. In Arjun Dangle (Ed.), *Poisoned Bread: Translations from Modern Marathi Dalit Literature* (pp. 322-334). Hyderabad: Orient Blackswan, 2011.

CHAPTER 5

Reflections on Female Madness in Literature

Dr. Priya Raghav and *Ms. Sarita*

Abstract

Throughout history women who have transgressed the boundaries assigned to them have been labelled as monsters, madwomen or witches. Moreover, the representations of such women in literature has been controlled by men. It is through male eyes that we see women who have become hysterical, insane or suicidal. In fact, madness was considered as a disease which was inherently feminine. It was not until the advent of psychiatry in the 19th century that a more humane approach was taken towards women who suffered from mental illnesses. How does literature reflect such women? Moreover, what is the relationship between women and madness? In this paper I will look at some of the most prominent literary instances of women who suffer from mental illness. We need to look deeper into such instances of mental health if we are to gain any concrete understanding on the subject. Today mental health is no longer a taboo subject. People are openly acknowledging their personal narratives in dealing with mental health issues. Since the outbreak of Covid issues surrounding mental health have once again been brought out of the closet. Dealing with instances of anxiety, depression, suicidal thoughts and loss have more support than ever as such instances have become widespread during the pandemic.

Keywords: madness, hysteria, melancholy.

Introduction

Madness has always fascinated literary critics and artists all over the world. During the Middle Ages and the Renaissance mad people were highly respected and revered. They were also regarded as healers who could cure many diseases. Yet the fear of the unknown or the unrepresentable made inroads into the way mad people were treated. The downward spiral continued till the nineteenth century when a more liberal view was taken of mad people. Over the centuries, madness became a gendered disease. Literature is replete with instances where women have become mentally deranged when they have transgressed societal norms or have tried to free themselves from the clutches of male hegemony. Women who cannot cope with the dictates of the society have only one available option and that is suicide. This is what Tolstoy's heroine does when her agony becomes unbearable. Anna Karenina is punished for having an extra marital affair with Vronsky. She begins living with Vronsky as his mistress. This is unacceptable to the elite Russian society. Anna is the fallen woman. A woman who has become a pariah. The double standards of the Russian society too are exposed. While Vronsky is accepted in his usual circles, Anna is not. Anna thus falls into what can be termed as a depressive state of mind. She is all alone with no friends. The author gives us a glimpse into her mental state just before she jumps to her death in front of a moving train. Anna also starts doubting the love of Vronsky though he reassures her repeatedly. The only way Anna can stop her torment is by committing suicide. A similar pattern can be seen in Gustav Flaubert's *Madame Bovary* (1856) and *Therese Raquin* (1873) by Emile Zola. Madame Bovary cannot bring herself to love her husband. She ends up ruining her marriage by having extra marital affairs. The only recourse available to her in the end is suicide. A similar fate awaits Therese Raquin, who plots to kill her husband with the help of her lover. In the end racked with guilt she commits suicide along with her lover. One wonders why suicide is the only recourse available for women who have transgressed the boundaries of what the society deems as 'proper'. Men on the other hand rarely seem to suffer from such manic-depressive states. Though not completely extinct, instances of men dealing with madness are sporadic.

How does one deal with a woman who can no longer fit in the society? Madness, hysteria, melancholy have always been closely associated with women. Hysteria was referred to as the female malady as early as 1900 BC. The etymology of the term hysteria can be traced to the Greek word hysteron which means womb. Hysteria refers to uncontrollable emotions. Though the exact cause of hysteria could not be ascertained, the reference to womb made it gender specific. Hysterical women have also been accused of suffering from demonic possessions. Quacks and witch doctors are always consulted when modern medicine fails to provide a cure for such neurotic diseases. Again, it is mostly women who suffer from such attacks by devils and vampires. Bram Stoker's famous novel *Dracula* (1897) attests to this as both Lucy and Mina suffer from psychological issues which manifest after their encounter with the Count.

Even literature meant for children is replete with examples of women who are witches. Snow White is threatened by her evil stepmother who is a witch. Hansel and Gretel are imprisoned by a witch before they finally escape. Sleeping Beauty is cursed by witch. These witches are powerful women who know the art of black magic. They have the power to cast spells. Whether it is the witches from *The Wizard of Oz* (1900) or the witches in *The Chronicles of Narnia* (1950), women who transgress the patriarchal society are isolated and treated as outcasts to say the very least. Moreover, as such women are deemed to be extremely powerful, they are accused of having supernatural powers. Women who cannot be controlled by men must be punished. A woman who is powerful is seen as a threat to patriarchy and the society in general. Women who are docile, submissive and weak are rewarded with rich husbands with whom they live happily ever after. Thus, young children especially girls are taught to be submissive and servile. Boys too are warned of the dangers inherent in allowing too much freedom or power to women. Women from tribal societies are also accused of practicing witchcraft and black magic.

One is immediately taken back to historical instances where women were labelled as witches and burnt at the stake, the most notable ones being that of the Spanish Inquisition and the Salem Witch trials. Witches were often known to indulge in pagan and ritualistic ceremonies. Exorcism of women who had become 'possessed' by the devil can be found in many religions. King James I had also written a book on demonology in 1597 and the Elizabethan stage was no stranger to this misogynistic portrayal of women. One of the sources of *Macbeth* (1606) was King James book. Macbeth meets his downfall when he listens to women who are powerful, perhaps more powerful and more ambitious than most men. The three witches prophesise that Macbeth will become the king. Why are these women called witches? Do they really have the power to look into the future?

Lady Macbeth is ambitious but once Duncan is murdered, she plunges into madness and finally commits suicide. She starts hallucinating that her hands are stained with blood and no matter how many times she washes her hands she cannot get the blood stains off. In *The Duchess of Malfi* (1613), the brothers of the widowed duchess warn her against remarriage. They want to become more powerful and rich by removing the duchess. When she stands up against her brothers she is captured, tortured and loses her mental balance before she is finally hanged.

In India women who are witches are also called *Dayans*. Myths surrounding witches are rampant, for example their reflection cannot be seen in the mirror and their feet are deformed. Edmund Spencer refers to witches in his epic *The Faerie Queene* (1590). Keats famous poem *La Belle Dame Sans Merci* (1819) warns us against women who are powerful enough to control men and refers to such women as witches.

Women are supposed to be inherently weak and therefore of unstable minds. A woman's testimony is and always has been questionable. In *The Passage to India* (1924) by E M Forester when Adela accuses Dr Aziz of assaulting her, she is confident that her version of the story will be accepted. Though Adela is a white woman her version of the story cannot be validated and the charges against Dr Aziz are dropped. A woman's story can always be dismissed and discredited as the ramblings of a madwoman.

Nineteenth Century Depictions of Madness

Nineteenth century England was witnessing powerful changes. It was a time of rapid industrialisation and progress. There was a shift from rural to urban spaces. The steam engine brought rapid changes in the life of the people. The changes were not confined to the economic state of England. There were scientific advancements as well. The doctors were looking at newer ways to treat patients, especially those who suffered from mental health issues. The way in which patients suffering from mental problems improved after the genesis of psychiatry in the early 1930s.

John Conolly a famous English psychiatrist refused to keep his patients in restraints and expressed his abhorrence towards the inhumane treatment of patients suffering from mental health issues. Philippe Pinel, another medic extended a more gentle treatment of such patients. American and English psychiatrists often collaborated with each other for the advancement of this particular field. Not only this but it became a matter of great pride for England when asylums were set up all over the country which were more humane in their treatment of such patients. Inspite of such rapid leaps women were not allowed to practice medicine and therefore the treatment of such patients was entirely in the hands of men. Elizabeth Blackwell became the first female psychiatrist in 1847. It is also pertinent to mention here that during the eighteenth century people who suffered from mental health issues were ostracised as they were regarded as criminals and idiots. In the nineteenth century however there was a shift in the general perceptions as mentally ill patients were now regarded as patients needing special care. The image of mentally ill patients changed from that of criminal idiots to that of the troubled females needing sympathetic treatment.

Female madness in literature of the age was personified by the triple images of *The Ophelia*, *The Crazy Jane* and *The Lucia*. While crazy Jane is referred to in many popular ballads Lucia was a female character in Gaetano Donizetti's 1835 opera, *Lucia of Lammermoor.* Lucia goes mad on her wedding day and murders the bridegroom. Of the three women mentioned Ophelia was the only servile and gentle one.

Nineteenth century representations of Ophelia saw her as the perfect Victorian madwoman, suffering from unrequited love. Hysteria became synonymous with the Ophelia syndrome. When studying Ophelia's madness, the psychiatrist J.C. Bucknill diagnosed her with love melancholy, noting that 'the loss of her lover [...] is uppermost in her thoughts [...] [N]ever was sentimental mania more truly and more exquisitely depicted than in [her character]'.

In different ways, Ophelia thus can be seen as a precursor of the Victorian fallen (mad)woman. Ophelia's story of seduction, rejection, madness and suicide corresponds to the narrative of the female stereotype retold again and again in the Victorian arts, and which could be seen to teach women an important moral, namely to adhere to the feminine ideal instituted by patriarchal ideology.

Victorian society's treatment of mad women is reflected in many literary examples. In Dickens, *The Great Expectations* (1860) we have the figure of Miss Havisham, a woman who is jilted on her wedding day. She has not changed anything from that day. Though she is now an old woman she continues to wear her wedding dress. Her room is exactly the way it was on her wedding day. She has adopted a girl called Estella. Miss Havisham wants Estella to break as many hearts as she can. In a way she is rallying against all men because she has been jilted.

Charlotte Bronte's epic bildungsroman *Jane Eyre* (1947) is often hailed as a feminist milestone. Yet if we read the novel more closely it is Bertha Mason, the mad wife of Edward Rochester who at once arrests our attention. Jane has often heard her 'mad' laughter. Bertha is represented as uncontrollable, fiendish, animalistic and therefore mad. When Rochester takes us to the third story of Thornfield Hall to give us a glimpse of Bertha Mason, she is uttering guttural sounds, she is down on all her fours like an animal and attacks Mr. Mason fiercely drawing blood. It is Jean Rhys who gives us the true story of Bertha Mason in *Wide Sargasso Sea* (1966) a prequel to *Jane Eyre* written almost a century later. Her name is not Bertha as we know but Antoinette, a Creole heiress. Rochester meets her in the Caribbean's and gets married to her for her money. Though he wants her money he is repulsed by her mixed heritage. Rochester looks for ways of denigrating his newly wed wife. He starts calling her Bertha instead of Antoinette. On numerous occasions he calls his wife a mad woman and an idiot. He also discovers that 'madness' runs in his wife's family. He goes back to England dragging the unfortunate Bertha with him. Uprooted from the only place she can call home, Bertha becomes a prisoner of Thornfield Hall under the watchful eyes of Grace Poole. Rochester now has complete control of Bertha and her fortune.

We learn of how Bertha acts like an arsonist trying to set fire to Rochester's bed in *Jane Eyre* (1847). Bertha also tears the wedding veil of Jane. She wants revenge from Rochester but unfortunately or perhaps conveniently for Rochester she falls to her death after setting Thornfield Hall on fire. We see how the figure of Bertha becomes a nemesis for Rochester. She represents a problem that cannot be wished away. Bronte removes her from the picture so that she can reunite Jane with Edward Rochester and give a happy ending to her novel. One wonders how the novel would have progressed had Bertha not jumped to her death.

The Angel/Monster divide referred to by Gilbert and Gubar is nowhere more evident than in the comparison between Bertha and Jane. Jane is gentle, docile and subservient. She is a perfect image of a perfect Victorian woman. Bertha on the other hand is wild, savage and uncontrollable. Jane is the angel and Bertha a monster. Yet there are similarities between Jane and Bertha. Jane too is wild, rebellious and uncontrollable. When we first meet Jane at Gateshead, she is just a child. Yet she is aware of the injustice meted out to her. Moreover, she questions authority at various points in life. She is aware of the hypocrisy inherent in the behavior of Mr. Brocklehurst when she is at Lowood. When Rochester first meets Jane, he thinks of her as a witch. Both, Jane and Bertha represent women who cannot be controlled. Thus we can draw parallels between Jane and Bertha though the two women meet very different ends.

The fact that women who did not conform to the standards set by the Victorian society were punished is emphasised in numerous other works of the era. Often such women were either stigmatised or labelled as insane. Nowhere is it more evident than in Wilkie Collins sensational novel *The Woman in White* (1851). Again, we come across the trope of feminine madness which is a recurrent image in the Victorian era. Anne Catherick is the illegitimate child of Mr. Fairlie. She is confined first by her own mother and later kept in an asylum. It is also implied that she has been abused as a child. Anne Catherick closely resembles Laura Fairlie, the heroine of the novel. We are introduced to Anne Catherick when she is running away from something fearful at night. She meets Walter Hartright on the way and warns him that he must stay away from Limmeridge House. Apparently, Anne Catherick has escaped from the asylum she was put in. Anne represents a threat to Sir Percival Glyde as she knows a secret. She also warns Laura about the true nature of Sir Percival Glyde. Though it is later discovered that she does not know any secret her fault lies in the fact that she stands up to Sir Percival. She meets an early death and is buried as Laura.

We see that death is the only recourse available for women who cannot be accepted by the society anymore. As she is the illegitimate daughter of Mr. Fairlie she has no position in the society. She is at the mercy of those who surround her. Lisa Appignanesi describes how the book: "illustrates rampant social fears about mistaken incarceration" and how "men in power can literally drive women mad, whether through marital sadism, drugs or sexual violation" (Appignanesi, 98). Here again we can see how Laura is the perfect Victorian heroine. She is submissive, weak, docile and gentle. Anne Catherick is insane and wild. Her version of the story cannot be validated as she has already been labelled as a mad woman. The only woman who is practical is Marion. Marion is instrumental in finding Laura and bringing the novel to its logical conclusion. She has no beauty and no money, therefore she resigns herself to a life of acting as a companion for Laura for the rest of her life.

Women writers have often reflected their personal experiences in their works. Charlotte Perkins Gilman's *The Yellow Wallpaper* (1892) is a semiautobiographical story of the author herself. She wrote the novel shortly after recovering from post-partum depression. The novel's protagonist suffers from a psychosis. Though she is sent to the countryside to recover she falls deeper into a depressive state. She starts imagining that there is a woman trapped in the yellow wallpaper and she is trying to get out. Finally the woman in the yellow wallpaper commits suicide. Gilman is trying to show us how women feel trapped in circumstances they want to avoid. The author sees the bars on her window as a state of being imprisoned. She is unable to cope with feelings of isolation, loneliness and despair. This worsens her state of mind.

Many women authors have suffered in silence from issues regarding mental health. Mary Wollstonecraft despite being an acclaimed feminist threw herself in the Thames in 1795, though she failed in her attempt to commit suicide. Virginia Woolf committed suicide by drowning herself in a river. Virginal Woolf wrote *A Room of One's Own* (1939) in which she emphasises how a woman can never really have any agency until she becomes economically independent. She also urges women writers to free themselves from the Angel/Monster binary. The angel in the house must be killed. Sylvia Plath too, a noted writer committed suicide at a very early age. She had a destructive relationship with her father. In her novel *The Bell Jar* (1963) Plath exposes a woman's descent into madness.

As more women write one can uncover more instances where women have suffered from psychological disorders. In Toni Morrison's novel *Beloved* (1987) one can see how Sethe suffers from the shackles of slavery. In a fit of insanity, Sethe kills her infant daughter as she does not want her daughter to suffer the way she has. She is later visited by the spirit of this very daughter whom she has named Denver. Again, in Morrison's novel *The Bluest Eye* (1970), Pecola the protagonist feels that she can become beautiful only if she has blue eyes. Thus, Morrison brings to light how race can become a factor in inflicting psychological trauma. Bessie Head was born in a mental asylum in South Africa. She was a product of miscegenation and her mother was not allowed to keep her. She was placed in foster care and her childhood was almost normal. Head went on to become a writer but she herself faced a severe bout of depression and she also tried to commit suicide. Though Head did not live long she is remembered for her works which establish her as a writer of repute.

In *The Joys of Motherhood* (1979) the central character Nnu Ego descends into madness and dies by the roadside after suffering throughout her life. The impact with colonisation changes her life forever. The traditional values are fractured and Nnu Ego cannot deal with the changed circumstances.

Aberrant women continue to suffer as misogynistic practices have not been completely erased. Education and science have tried to dispel superstitions surrounding female madness, hysteria and witch craft. Yet such representations of women continue to flourish in films, urban legends, folk lore and literature. Perhaps it is the thrill of the unknown or the unrepresentable that continues to keep such images alive in human memory. Of course, feminist critics have blamed patriarchy and male hegemony for such portrayals of women. Tennessee Williams representation of Blanche Du Bois, the mentally deranged sister of Stella in *A Streetcar Named Desire* (1947) is unforgettable. Blanche is accused of having an affair with her student and of prostitution. Finally she is sent to an asylum. Whatever may be the reason, challenges to mental health continue to this day and hopefully a more enlightened view will emerge as more research goes into the field.

Conclusion

Mental health remains a matter of concern as we become more technology driven and our social life takes a back seat. Literature is replete with instances of characters grappling with mental health issues. Whether it is Dario Fo's depiction of the madman in *The Accidental Death of an Anarchist* (1970) or the nearly insane protagonists of Samuel Beckett's famous play *Waiting for Godot* (1952), representations of men and women dealing with psychological issues continue to flourish in literature. Shakespeare's *Hamlet* (1601) is perhaps the most famed literary example of a person suffering from borderline neurosis. Post-World War II instances of madness were on the rise. Septimus Warren Smith cannot get over the war and finally commits suicide in *Mrs. Dalloway* (1925). Instances of existential angst, alienation and anxiety became more frequent as one started questioning the meaning of life and the existence of God. Writers like Nietzsche proclaimed that God is dead. As the horrors of the war unfolded the very foundations of religious beliefs were shattered.

Children were orphaned, women were widowed and old people were left with no one to care for them. This pattern has been historically repeated numerous times.

At times madness is also thought of as something amusing. One cannot forget the hilarious way in which Cervantes portrays his mad protagonist, Don Quixote. We need to look more closely at such instances to reach at the root cause of such problems. Of course, one does wonder if issues relating to mental health are here to stay. We as a society need to take a more humane outlook towards people suffering from mental health issues.

Women's mental health in particular continues to pose challenges even today. Wars, ethnic oppression, poverty, patriarchy, political repression and pandemics are among the factors that can lead to psychological problems. In fact, diseases like bipolar disorder, schizophrenia, multiple personality disorder are more common today than ever. Feelings of alienation and loneliness that result from such disorders are well documented. It is not just women but also men who suffer from such diseases though the percentage may vary. The diseases can be traced back to mental trauma suffered by the victim at any given point of time. The stigma associated with such problems needs to be removed. They are just like any other ailment a person can suffer from. As more research goes into psychological disorders, doctors are confident of treating such patients, curing them completely.

Works Cited

Appignanesi, L. Mad, Bad and Sad. *A History of Women and the Mind Doctors from 1800 to the Present.* 2008. London: Virago Press. Print.

Bucknill, John Charles, *The Psychology of Shakespeare.* London: Longman, Brown, Green, Longmans & Roberts, 1859. Print

Chesler, Phyllis. *Women and Madness.* 2nd ed. New York: Four Walls Eight Windows, 1997. Print.

Showalter, Elaine. *The Female Malady: Women, Madness, and English Culture,* 1890-1980. London: Penguin Books, 1987. Print.

Gilbert, Sandra M, and Susan Gubar. *The Madwoman in the Attic: The Woman Writer and the Nineteenth-Century Literary Imagination.* New Haven: Yale University Press, 2000. Print.

"Hysteria." Oxford English Dictionary. 2018. http://www.oed.com/.

CHAPTER 6

Rabindranath Tagore's *Chokher Bali*: A Precursor to Womanhood

Dr. Sonali Mahanta

Abstract

The concept of *women and identity* in the context of Indian literature during the beginning of the 19th century could be well explored with Rabindranath Tagore's *Chokher Bali*. The setting of the novel is Bengal, but the status of the woman has got pan Indian implications as well as suggestions. This novel majorly explores the complex interpersonal niche of the female protagonist Binodini and her triangulated aspirations. Apart from this, it also delves into the stringent rules for a widow in Indian society during the 19th century. Binodini, Rajalakshmi along with Annapurna are three major widow female characters in the novel, who constantly express their inner desires. *Chokher Bali* is about how they are denied their attainments by the world due to the invalid reasons for which they are not even responsible.

Chokher Bali rejoices the inner self of Binodini and resurfaces the suppressed desire of a young widow and there lies no irrationality to that. The novel bestows on two interacting surfaces such as societal obligations and personal preferences. The society where Binodini survived, expects a lady to pass with the flow of the existing time and thereby ignore her humanly existence. The prevailing norms of society have not only severely degraded but also damaged a woman's position. This enforces them to obey the patriarchal demands as well as to denounce all the pleasures of life and settle down with a minimal level of survival. Hence, Tagore's contemporary period was suggestive of a minimalist approach to a widow's survival and avoidance of all affinity and affiliations of the female self. It almost spaces a widow as an infected part of the society with no social, economical, or emotional rights. Hence, this paper is trying to scan through the disgruntled nature of society toward a widow during the 19th century. For doing so, it has taken the help of charactorial as well as the instantial details of the novel.

Keywords: Womanhood, societal restriction, minimalist approach, degraded position, subservient

Introduction

The sorrow, suffering, and penance of a young widow get intensified by society's further forceful restrictions and it's not peculiar to that period but is everlasting. But the only contrast is that the majority of the present lady hardly pay any attention to such derogatory remarks and goes on fulfilling their dreams. The current novel explores the character Binodini, who is a young widow. It features multiple relations of Binodini such as an extramarital affair with Mahendra, her friendship with Asha, her true fascination for Bihari, and her complex friendship with Asha. Tagore substantiates the temporariness of human relationships through psychological interplays. There are several other themes, that *Chokher Bali* voices such as the status of women's education as well as literacy in the society, the matter of equal rights, the dominance of patriarchal society, the issue of child marriage, and above all the treatment of the society with the widows.

Chokher Bali is a colloquial word in Bengali that means an *irritant to the eye*. Two young friends Binodini and Asha are irritants to each other's eyes. The writer documents certain humanly attributes as well as sentiments for developing the novel such as a human craving for the fulfilment of their desires, satiating the ego, envy, unhappiness, intolerance, tactful persuasions, infidelity, immorality, half-heartedness, deception, arrogance, lie, unreliability, greed and many more. The current analysis has been done with a couple of sections such as a literature review and a section on the analysis of the novel concerning several themes, but primarily the question of womanhood. The section on analysis highlights the contrast between the social demands and a young widow's aspirations. It leads to the point that how societal obligations compelled a young widow to sacrifice her choices and preferences to survive as a dignified soul. Truly, Tagore's role in the liberation of women is a seminal one. *Chokher Bali* is one such work which not only represents the plight of the women but also argued for their deserved rights. Through the concerned novel, Tagore has constructed an epoch-making character of Binodini, which has added to the evolution of female characters and their rightful existences as well.

Seema (2011), designates *Chokher Bali* as a norm defying novel. She further elaborates that the novel scans into the multiple aspects of human relationships and instantiates how certain decisions result in a disharmonious life. She also adds that jealousy and deprivation of happiness can make a human being forget all human ties and relationships. According to Gupta, (2019) Tagore's novel *Chokher Bali* sits on lust, jealousy, entangled fate and sacrifices. He mentioned that the novel takes us to visualise a Bengali household. According to Finru (2003), *Chokher Bali* narrates the story of four young people trapped in a tangle of sensuality. According to him, it entails the saga of rejection and revenge that led to the tragic passage of the female protagonist Binodini herself.

According to Hoque (2019), the central character Binodini is far from the so-called idealised Indian woman. She has been projected with shades of grey and humanly flaws. Binodini became a widow at a very young age and thus constantly struggles for the satiation of her wishes and desires. She further mentions that Tagore has provided scope for the readers to gain an insight into her desires. Tarafdar (2019), analyses it as a novel with a strong female protagonist that can imprint indelible marks in the memory lane. According to Chatterjee (2003), *Chokher Bali* belongs to the literature of the new age, which unravels the secrets of the true heart. In his words, "the female protagonist Binodini is a full-blooded young widow stifled by social restrictions while articulating the legitimate anguish of an unwitting victim of adverse circumstances and the rigours of the dowry system".

Summarily, Tagore has carried forward the message for the upliftment of socio-cultural needs and ways for the betterment of women in the 19th century. All types of social stigmas and inappropriateness are traditionally employed to exploit the female sex. Tagore has openly disseminated the 19th-century female condition through his artistic brilliance and covered topics such as woman education, social and economic rights and above all a just accommodation in the male-dominated patriarchal society.

A Critical Analysis

This section attempts an analysis of the novel with a special focus on the projections of womanhood with the help of certain traits. The concept has been elaborated into two sub-sections. The first sub-section deals with the list of characters both male as well as female. The second sub-section delves into the societal obligations and personal preferences of the female protagonist Binodini. This section tries to display the contrasting attitude of Binodidni toward the societal demands and her endeavour to settle down on a reconciliatory point with the issue and expectations of her contemporary society.

The novel has got a multitude of characters but the story heavily revolves around five major characters such as Binodini (the female protagonist), Mahendra (who has extramarital affair with Binodini), Ashalata (Binodini's friend and Mahendra's young wife), Bihari (Mahendra's adopted brother), and Rajlakshmi (Mahendra's mother). contributors to every single plot and contribute to the organic development of the theme. Few other supporting characters are Annapurna (sister-in-law of Rajlakshmi), Ashalata's maternal aunt, Swarna, Manorama, the woman accompanying the English missionary, a young courtesan.

One of the major traits of the play is that non of the characters are completely flat or round. Flat characters signify a character which is devoid of any complexity, whereas, round characters are portrayed with multifarious traits. As per the characters of the *Chokher Bali* are concerned most of the characters are a mixture of both straight as well as complicated behaviour. The characters are mostly with apt humanly attributes and rightfully in affinity with worldly emotions such as love, hatred, jealousy, revenge and many more. For instance, the female protagonist Binodini has been endowed with humanly attributes like ambition, jealousy, and rebellion. Similarly, the character of Bihari has been portrayed with features like calmness, poise and sympathy. Mahendra is carefree, adamant and ignores others' emotions. He does whatever suits him. Ashalata, wife of Mahendra is opposite of him. She is docile and submissive and readily agrees to sacrifice her desires for her husband.

Most of the time, social obligations and personal preferences are poles apart and are ever-widening gaps. Society has its norms in every phase of history and is mostly regulated by patriarchal ideas. Societal obligations concern the *duties* or *commitments* which are legally or morally bound to do something. Writer (2020) defines social obligation as the need to do something entrenched to formalised social etiquette. This topic relates to Binodini's character as well as Rajalakshmi and Annapurna, who disinterestedly keep on observing all the customs and rituals that a widow should observe as per the so-called social conventions. Not only Binodini but Rajalakshmi as well as Annapurna repeatedly expresses their sorrow of being a widow, as they have to restrain themselves to participate in any of the ceremonies. For instance,

Rajalakshmi can't even welcome her only daughter in law due to such prevailing customs as the shadow of a widow, on a newlywed has been considered to be an ill omen. On the contrary, as Binodini was a convent educated lady, neither she fully denied carrying out the practices nor expressed her indifference to the same. The character of Binodini largely reflects the plight of the widows of the 19th century.

According to Stacy (2020), "the 19thcentury widows existed on the fringes of society and were disallowed from enjoying any of the regular comforts of life like sleeping on a bed, eating delicious food, and wearing colourful clothes, or even having hair". She further elaborates that this kind of life would incite a certain amount of bitterness in them and would be entirely accurate. Hence, Binodini after getting widowed was under the thought process that she deserves all that went to Ashalata, which guzzled a revengeful attitude in her towards Ashalata. She tried manipulating every person which in some way or the other is linked to Mahendra. Nevertheless, she also becomes successful in that. She also starts persuading Mahendra's mother against Ashalata and got successful to some extent. All these started when Mahendra's mother left her house and went to the village where Binodini was living, to teach a lesson to Mahendra. Binodini took utmost care of his mother and developed an intimate relationship with his mother. As a result, while returning to Kolkata Rajlakshmi decided to take Binodini back to Kolkata.

Binodini was down with some other hidden and unhealthy intentions. She has a superiority complex which charged the wrong intentions in her. She compared her beauty, musical skills, education and other day-to-day competencies with that of Asha and establishes herself in a higher place. Binodini also started developing a friendliness towards Ashalata to get closer to Mahendra. She also emerges victorious with the same and becomes successful in developing a romantic relationship with Mahendra. At the same time, Binodini has true love feelings for Bihari. Binodini through her tactics convinced Mahendra that she is superior to Ashalata in every context of life say it be her education, looks or household affairs. Gradually, Binodini and Ashalata became irritants to the eyes of each other.

Tagore's *Chokher Bali* truly places the characters true to their lives and genuinely portrays the worldly senses added with realistic depictions. Rajlakshmi, Binodini, Mahendra, Bihari, and Ashalata are all enacted as real-life characters. Binodini who initially was blinded by revenge has transformed into a sensible character. Ashalata transformed herself into a more confident character with the advancing situations.

Conclusion

In conclusion, Binodini is not very appreciative of leading her life as a widow, as she is still very young. She survived in such an era that considers female education to be an omen and remains unappreciative of it. Binodini is also way ahead of such mentalities and with such liberal thoughts, it becomes difficult for her to survive in the orthodox society. Her freedom of speech and thought made her away from all rehabilitation in the later phase of her life. This worldly perception and her calculations were encountered quite several times. She is a well-informed lady and her ideology is a sharp contrast to that of the prevailing, accepted as well as followed norms. Thereby, towards the climax, she reconciles her revolting soul to some extent to the situational demands that might reserve a secured position in society. It could be said that *Chokher Bali* engenders the emergence of a new form of womanhood, who is very keen on setting their goals as well as fulling their desires.

Works Cited

Chatterjee, M. N. *Indian Literature*, vol. 48, no. 2 (220), 2004, pp. 182–85, http://www.jstor.org/stable/23341277. Accessed 18 May 2022.

Fainru, D. 27th August 2003. *Chokher Bali: A Passion Play*. Retrieved from https://www.screendaily.com/chokher-bali-a-passion-play/4014714.article

Gupta, M. (28TH August 2019). *Chokher Bali By Rabindranath Tagore*. A Timeless Classic Of Love Lust And Loneliness. Ecstatic Yet Chaotic.

Hoque, N.[February 15, 2019]. *Book Review: Chokher Bali – A Grain Of Sand By Rabindranath Tagore*. Feminism in India.

https://feminisminindia.com/2019/02/15/chokher-bali-rabindranath-tagore-review/#:~:text=The%20novel%20explores%20the%20extramarital,play%20%2C%20but%20most%20importantly%20presents

Seema. [March 11, 2021]. *Rabindranath Tagore's Norm-Defying Novel, Chokher Bali. Owlcation*. Retrieved from https://owlcation.com/

Stacy, [31st October 2020]. *What happened in Chokher Bali?*. Retrieved from

https://www.bookseriesrecaps.com/what-happened-in-chokher-bali/

Tarafdar, S. [February 20, 2019]. *Book Review: Chokher Bali by Rabindranath Tagore.*

https://www.womensweb.in/2019/02/book-review-chokher-bali-by-rabindranath-tagore/

Writer, S. [April 08, 2020]. *What Is the Definition of "social Obligation"?*

https://www.reference.com/world-view/definition-social-obligation-2b442d6f2e8bda36

CHAPTER 7

Patriachal Society and Gender Power – A Critical Analysis of *The Palace of Illusion* by Chitra Divakaruni

Dr B. Chandana

Abstract

"The Palace of Illusion" is a novel of historical fiction delineating one of the two great epics of Hindus, "The Mahabharata". The author of the book, Chitra Banerjee Divakaruni is a sixty-three year old Indo-American author with a Master's degree in English from Wright University of United States. The present book is a historical fiction that narrates the story of "The Mahabharata" from the time of the genesis of Panchaali or Draupadi, the daughter of King Drupadi. The story evolves round her while exploring the then patriarchal world and its happenings. The book is a reflection of the society of its kings and queens and the reflection of their psychology. The research paper highlights of woman living in a patriarchal world and Gender power structure through the character of Draupdi.

Keywords: patriarchal society, gender power, life of women, element of fate, power structure

Introduction

Chitra Banerjee Divakaruni is the writer of the book "The Palace of Illusion" – based on the Indian epic Mahabharat. Chitra an Indian born America is a well-known poet, writer and activist. Her published works bring out her love for Indian mythology. The Palace of Illusion was written in the year 2008, in an era seen as emergence of women power. The novel is a beautiful narration of the emotions of a lonely yet brave princess who has a secret attraction towards a mysterious man no other than one of her husband's ferocious enemy (Keerthana,. 2019).

An Analysis of the Patriarchal World and the Life of Women

The novel starts with the reminiscences of Panchaali narrating her genesis. It tells about the deepest desire of King Drupadi who goes on to making prayers to gods for over a period of thirty days after which he finds his wish fulfilled. The craving for a child is not anything rare in the Indian historical contexts but it refers to the culture of ascension of throne to be made by only a prince and a king must have an heir to govern his state. The trend is tremendously patriarchal and the same mindset is present in the history of other nation too. The marriage of a girl, in a patriarchal society, is one of the ancient aspects reflected in the book (Panda, 2019).. It depicts the society where the marriage of women go independent of their likes and dislikes. In other words, the marriage of Panchaali absolutely depends on the results of the archery tournament arranged by King Drupadi. According to the arrangements whosoever becomes successful in piercing the eyes of a fish moving on the ceiling without directly looking at it can marry Panchaali. Karna becomes successful in doing so but he fails to supply details of his parental identity and faces sheer humiliation by her amid all present at the tournament (Sapkota, 2019). Later Arjuna appears in the disguise of a Brahmin and wins the tournament. Upon the suggestion of the mother of the Pandavas, Panchaali became the wife of all other four brothers too. This incident too shows that the women used to enjoy almost no freedom in making decision on their marriage. Later she has children by all five of her husbands.

The clash of the Kauravas and the Pandavas too is nothing but the patriarchal mindset of chivalry and readiness to sacrifice life for a wrong reason of showing their gallantry. Their great grandfather and the son of the goddess Ganges, Bheesma makes separate accommodation for the Pandavas in Indraprastha. Maya builds a palace with optical illusions so rampant that anyone can face the challenge of identifying the real from the illusory ones. Maya arranges the flow of water inside the palace upon the request of Panchaali. Maya warns the Pandavas about the potential risk of the optical illusion for which they should never invite anyone in their palace. Things starts going on smooth until one day Duryodhan, the eldest of the one hundred sons and a daughter of the Kauravas apper. The illusory palace makes him fall in the water only to get laughed at by the maids of Panchaali. The humiliation faced by him does not allow him to rest and he goes on devising plan against the Pandavas. The fate of Kirna and Panchaali begins to unfold right from this moment, unknown of the future events to happen in their lives both think about the situation in two different ways.

As an evil spirit Duryodhan plays trick in the game of dice and makes Yudhistir, the eldest of the Pandavas, lose everything one by one. As he decides to go on playing the game, he loses jewels, palace, and becomes Duryodhan's slave (Dhakal, 2017). The game goes to such an extent that he has to place their wife Panchaali as bet only to lose and get utterly humiliated. The incident shows that women do not have a say on their own selves but their husbands and father at different stages of their life. Prior to her marriage King Drupad decides the affairs even when it is as serious as an affair like marriage when Panchaali remains a silent victim of the patriarchal society and its mindset. Putting her as bet in the game of dice shows the same barbaric mindset which allows considering women of that time as mere properties or commodities easily disposable on the whims of the husband.

The pre-planned game delivered the much desired victory to the Kauravas. Dussasan, the younger brother of Duryodhan, finds no barrier in taking revenge of the humiliation Duryodhan faced in the palace of illusion and brings Pachaali dragging in the hall where no one dares to protect the respect of a woman. All the warriors and elderly people reputed for their justice go silent amid which Duryodhan demands the humiliating demand to have her on her lap. However, Sri Krishna saves her from losing her respect any further. It shows the same mindset of the patriarchal society considering a woman a mere property men can unleash the vilest of wrong-desires (Chakraborty, 2018). The silence of the men, even when injustice continues, shows that a woman can suffer the fate for which she does not have any control than undergoing the humiliation and injury. The war of Kurukshetra begins and Panchaali loses all her sons, during which nightmares and nightmarish experiences become her regular companion. The Pandavas win the battle but with a heavy price of losing near and dear ones.

The entire book shows that Panchali has to make the largest amount of sacrifice as she suffers the bereavement of losing her sons too. The description by the author becomes vivid and makes the reader aware of the contemporary world where the continuation of the same psychological trait sustains only in changed shape and form.

The novel makes the readers aware of the analogy of the pain and pathos of Panchaali and the millions of women who relentlessly engage themselves into a never-ending battle seeking the basic right – the right to make their own decisions in every sphere of life without making compromise for self-respect.

A deeper look into the incidents take place as mentioned in the book introduces the readers to the story of Panchaali as one single character who suffered the most. Right from the beginning the imbalance of rights between the men and the women become vivid. Marriage, being one of the most significant happenings, Panchaali remains deprived of her right to make her own choice (Sharmila, 2020). She has to depend on the arrangements prepared by her father, Drupad. The very sense of not having the right to choose her own life-partner shows the first onslaught on the fundamental rights of women. She is a victim of traditional patriarchal system in which women do not have right to make major decisions of life. Her sufferings continue through her acceptance of four more brothers apart from Arjuna. The readers fall at their wit's end when they find that another woman, Kunti, the mother of the Pandavas takes the brutal decision for Panchaali to have all five brothers as her husbands. The decision made by Kunti works like a shock and makes the readers feel to ponder over the system which makes a woman to think and decide such a thing while depriving another woman of her rightful life. Kunti too is a result of the patriarchal system which makes her wipe out the usual feelings to the pain of another woman, Panchaali. The incident shows that Pachaali does not have the option to seek refuge under Kunti when she needs a motherly woman. Thr orle of Kunti, though does not play much in the book, clearly shows the horridness of the system which makes her think and act most unwomanly. The helplessness of Panchaali remains unheard throughout the novel with only occasional exceptions when gets responded by Sri Krishna.

Partiarchy is social system in which man hold main power in social and family system. "Sita's Ramayana" by Sanhita Arni is a book that narrates the familiar story of another Hindu epic "The Ramayana". The book is a retelling of the "The Ramayana" from the perspective of Sita, the wife of Rama. The cruelty of the patriarchal society becomes vivid throughout the sufferings of Sita too. Though Sita does not have to marry more than one prince, she suffers a different fate for which she has to undergo ordeals to prove her sanctity as a wife. Panchaali never faces the challenges thrown at her raising questions on her chastity but she suffer innumerable episodes of humiliation by the Kauravas, essentially representing all the vice of the patriarchal society. "The Palace of Illusions" reflects the patriarchal society captured in "The Mahabharata" of Dwapara Yuga (31032 BCE) while the pathos of Sita originally found in "The Ramayana" of Treta Yuga. The difference of yugas fail to show any affirmative changes in the status of women while the control of the society remains solely in the hands of men irrespective of their vice and virtues (Debnath, 2020). A woman has comparatively less power than man that can make her life miserable in context of various day-to-day as well complex situations. It was male dominated society even in ancient India and situation is very improved in modern India. However, Indian society is still male dominating. Various part of India still denies women' rights and make them vulnerable to domestic violence.

The character of Pachaali is the embodiment of struggle and sufferings. The game of thrones proves that Panchaali is nothing more than mere commodity. She is the universal embodiment of suffering womanhood continuing from time immemorial. She suffers the pathos of the sufferings of a woman, a wife and a mother too. The absence of right of Panchaali is still in the society whenever there is an incident of forcing a woman. During the period when the Pandavas has to live in disguise in a neighboring palace and Panchaali as a maid, Panchaali has to face Prince Keechak who threatens her of raping.

The more she undergoes humiliation and sufferings the more the possibilities of a massive change in the character of Pachaali becomes inevitable (Dalessandro, 2018). It is before the battle of Kurukshetra, she starts having terrible nightmares of death and loss. But she learns to ignore all the ominous signs expressed in her nightmares and declares her husbands should put an end to the tyranny of the Kaurava, led by Duryodhan. Shee too moulds her character with the same indifference to other's suffering, arrogance of challenging death for every second issue and of all which makes her suffer in silence and deep within herself. The patriarchal society, as depicted in the book, is so overpowering that it terminates all possibilities of being a woman with all her womanish feelings and outlooks to life. The incidents told in "The Palace of Illusion" makes the readers think of the present-day world and find the epic-struggle for securing the recognition of the womanhood for being what they are while remaining free from all the tiring-burdens of expectations.

The author introduces Panchaali as the narrator and she goes on retelling her life. Her life showcases the life of women under the absolute leadership of men making the society think and act the way men wants. There is a clear distinction between men and women for chivalry and absolute right embodies in men when women represents pawns beautiful and worth possessing the way men want. Panchali has some education at her paternal home but remains deprived of formal education. Being a woman she loses her right to learn the use of weapons. She does not get the right to join war as she has no formal education on warfare (Kaur, 2017). It refers to the fundamental mindset of the male-governed society which considers women too soft to make such daring acts. Critics say that Panchaali belongs to a royal dynasty for which her character may lack the overall representation of the women in the entire society. The character of Panchaali is the universal embodiment of pain and pathos of entire womankind irrespective of time and place.

Analysis of The Structure of Gender-power and the Element of Fate

Her fate has always overpowered her dreams and desires. In her entire life cycle, she experiences a varied mix of emotions like humiliation, unconditional love, devotion, power, revenge and forgiveness. But at every stage, her fate and destiny controls the sequence of events. Draupadi and her brother Dhristadhyumna are believed to be born out of the sacrificial fire yagna performed by their father Draupada. Panchaali has a lonely childhood with her brother being her sole confidant and friend. Draupada wanted the best groom for Panchaali and therefore arranges a Swayamvara inviting the brave Princes'. Karn the illegitimate son of Rani Kunti participates in ceremony but falling in the hands of fate, Panchaali disapproves him because of his mysterious progeny.

As destined, Arjuna wins the swayamvara and marries Panchaali. However the destiny once again takes an ugly turn for Panchaali and she has to accede to the orders of Arjuna and choose to become the wife of all the five pandava brothers. As the story unfolds, Panchaali is depicted as a strong woman who fearlessly questions her husband Yudhisthra in public when he loses her in the game of dice. She is a woman with unconditional patience even worked as a maid for the love of her family. As an egoist princess, she does not hesitate in insulting the fierce Duryodhana. Born out of fire, she has can be dangerous to extent of taking Kichak's life for challenging her modesty and respect. Grey shades of revenge are also seen in her character.

As a whole Panchaali is a best depiction of woman in today's world. There is a little Panchaali in every woman. These similarities are seen not only in their characters but also in actions. Today's world remains a man dominated society which at regular intervals gives little concessions to women choices corresponding to the Swayamvara, the decision making power elite women had in times of Mahabharat (Premalatha, et.al. 2020).

Sadly the fate of women in the contemporaries' societies of the world is still decided by men. Inequalities of men and women still persist in modern world. Inequality of gender has already been described as in Mahabharata Kaal. Drapuadi had to suffer due to gender inequality. As fathers, brothers and spouses they are still challenging the women's cognitive intelligence. Panchaali's father was the man behind organising the Swayamwara, a father's desire to choose the mightiest for her daughter. Panchaali's emotions and desires were of no importance. Panchaali's patience is worth mentioning. Working as a maid in the last year of their agyatvaas, she suffered insults at various instances without even uttering a single word. The women of today have to suffer a lot of humiliation in the competitive world. They are labelled feminist for raising their voices, their ambition is misunderstood as power hungry and career oriented. The situations have not changed greatly from the times of Mahabharat. The example of Panchaali revenging Prince Kichak sets a classic moral lesson for increasing crime against women in the recent times. The women have to take charge and become strong to oppose any challenges and attacks intended to their modesty. Panchaali was a powerful woman, extremely beautiful and virtuous. Her spiritual aura was divine. Inspite of being the wife of brave monarchs, she never let her devotion for Lord Krishna go weak. It is the beliefs that make us bounce back in hard times. Our beliefs and undiluted faith keep us afloat in the seas of sorrows.

Critics hold Panchaali responsible for the battle between Kauravas and Pandavas. The enmity could have been avoided had she not rejected and criticized Duryodhana. This is so true even today, we hear women being raped and murdered on accounts of rejecting the advances of their so called lovers. The struggle and desire of a woman in order to her gain respect and dignity is still present in the modern times.

Panchaali experiences all kinds of possible situations a woman can go through in her life starting from a fiery birth, secret love, submission to husband's will, central power, humiliation, revenge, forgiveness, motherhood, affection, devotion etc. Her action in each situation is largely guided by the destiny that was written even before her birth (Panda, Madhulika. 2019). Krishna explains Panchaali that the reason for every suffering in her present life holds relevance to her previous birth. Her fate steers her life at every turn.

She finds solace in the devotion of Lord Krishna. Her beliefs and devotion give her the power to emerge as a winner in her life. The same holds true in the present situation as well. Fate and destiny decide how a person acts in these situations. It is the beliefs and notions that the person holds gives strength to emerge in situations and fulfill the reason for their

All major human civilisations leave a track of the existence of gender power at some point or the other of their existence. The society depicted throughout the great epic of "The Mahabharata" too does not show any deviation. The building blocks of the society remain families when women sit in the epicenter of the each family subject to the willingness and directions of the men. The women remaining subjects of bearing child and gratifying carnal desires of the men, they do not have the access to weaponry and other activities like governing the country, (Chakraborty, 2018). The women remains oppressed and cannot make their own decisions. Lack of power to make decision for her own life pushes her to live a dissatisfied life. In other words, Gender power is considered main cause of poor quality life or higher rate of depression among women across world. During her maiden life, a woman has to follow the directions of her father including the right to choose her own husband. The society remains entirely divided into two discrete segments – the men and the women. The men takes care of all the affairs to governing the state, warfare, participating in various games with abundant use of free-will while the women remain in the possession of men (Lissy and Sivaranjani, 2018). The society considers them as objects – useful in taking care of domestic affairs including giving birth to desirably male children and being used as pawns if needed. However incredible may it sound the status of women gets well-reflected in the character of Panchaali or Draupadi, the daughter of King Drupad and who later becomes the wife of the Pandavas. The humiliation faced by her and the sufferings caused to her proves the same. It is the misuse of the gender-power which goes on creating a very long series of inhuman experiences all through her life. Moreover, the blatant use of the power brings about the epic-war killing almost the entire Kauravas. The element of fate remains overpowering all the actions of the characters in the epic. The arrangements made by King Drupad, the father of Panchaali, for choosing her groom is a complex paradigm of the perception of control. Panchaali, under the arrangements of her father King Drupad wants to make the decision of choosing a suitable groom. Karna gets rejected as he does not belong to any royal dynasty and then Arjuna, one of the Pandavas, qualify the ordeal and marries her. They have a perceived-control over the marriage when the marriage remains a pre-destined affair. Duryodhan, the eldest of the Kauravas, too think of in control of his destiny but his arrogance bringing about their destruction remains in the hands of fate. Sage Vyasa, Narada, Sri Krishna and other great rishis remains aware of the happenings much earlier than they actually take place. The battle of Kurukshetra remains a fight for dharma and the defeat of sinners is only a matter of time. Each and every single incident depicted in the epic remains in the perfect alignment of establishing dharma even when both sides book loss of property and life.

Conclusion

The book claims its relevance in many ways. The familiar story of The Mahabharata when retold from the perspective of a woman written by a woman author it becomes an epicenter of attraction for the readers. It allows a unique opportunity to see the same world from the different point of view or the point of view of a woman. The protagonist of the book remains Panchaali and knowing the incidents from her narratives make it worth reading. The status of women irrespective of their lineage bears the singularity of oppression and humiliation for innumerable times. The gender discrimination and access to rights become vivid and the readers cannot help express empathy with her. The role of fate too is evident and a careful reading with frequent linking of incidents shows that how destiny remains operational amid all decisions and incidents where the men remain under the wrong perception that they control their fate. Here the role of fate is not what the Greek tragedies and Shakespearean tragedies depict but it goes functional in a different way, as the concept of tragedy does not go befitting with the epic or any of its character. The entire set of incidents remains pre-destined for the establishment of dharma.

Works Cited

Chakraborty, Prasanta. "Shades of Violence in The Palace of Illusions-A Critical Study." *Language in India* 18.3 (2018).

Dalessandro, Cristen. "'Sister'and 'brother'schools, women and men: gender, power and inequality in a women's college space." *Journal of Gender Studies* 27.8 (2018): 969-980.

Debnath, Kakoli. "A Critique of the "Politics of Ideology" In Divakaruni's The Palace of Illusions." *Studies in Indian Place Names* 40.60 (2020): 3652-3663.

Erney, Hans-Georg. "Draupadi returns with a vengeance." *Journal of Postcolonial Writing* 55.4 (2019): 486-497.

Keerthana, V., and I. I. M. A. English. "Transcending Grand Narratives–A Study of Chitra Divakaruni's The Palace Of Illusions as a Re-telling of Mahabharata." *Language in India* 19.1 (2019).

Kumar, Ugresh. "A Historical Study of Women in India." *Our Heritage* 68.1 (2020): 564-578.

Lissy, R., and R. Sivaranjani. "Immigrant Feminine Experience in the Select Novels of Chitra Banerjee Divakaruni." *Language in India* 19.7 (2019).

Panda, Madhulika. "Chitra Banerjee Divakaruni's The Palace of Illusions: Mythology Reconstructed." *IUP Journal of English Studies* 14.3 (2019): 51-56.

Premalatha, S., and Puja Gadhave. "Voiceless Women in Mythology-An Analysis of Sita and Draupadi." *Our Heritage* 68.30 (2020): 12301-12312.

Sharmila, S. "Draupadi as an objectified and dehumanised woman in Chitra Banerjee Divakaruni's The Palace of Illusions." *Language in India* 20.1 (2020).

Sørensen, Siri Øyslebø. "Women to the rescue?: Gender, power and idealism in the third sector." *Bodies, Symbols and Organisational Practice. Routledge*, 2017. 167-186.

Suryawan, Nashrul Wahyu, and Vivi VW Damayanti. "The Representation of Women in the Rajagopalachari's Version of "Mahabharata" as the "Garwa" in the Javanese Culture Perspective." *International Journal of Linguistics, Literature and Translation* 2.2 (2019): 290248.

CHAPTER 8

Of Wounded Souls: Female Body through Manto's Lens

Dr. Salma Javed

Abstract

Sadat Hasan Manto belonged to the Progressive Writers Association. Writers belonging to this association made a point to incorporate the extreme need to discuss gender along with sexual politics in their works. The topics of concern for this group were sexuality, gender injustice, patriarchy and sadism. Literary works full of such ahead of the time subjects were smashed in the face of the patriarchy by these writers fearlessly. These writers tried to bring to light the feminist analytics that was usually kept in the backdrop or were not considered worth discussing. Their work examined the females of the society that had to bear the violence of all sorts. All along their writing journey, they tried to ensure a sustaining faith and a just temperament with which they wished the world to see women. Manto wrote about the incidents taking place in society, the brutal conditions prevailing during the partition era, the hypocrisy that existed in those times and the discriminatory attitudes. This paper has attempted to discuss a short story, *Hatak*, written by Manto, concerning society's two-facedness and how women were considered mere objects.

Keywords: Patriarchy, partition women, feminism, sexuality, hypocrisy.

Introduction

Writers from different generations have tried to explore female nature and their role in society. Several literary pieces discuss how our country was politically liberated during the twentieth century. Very few discuss how the women of our nation were subjected to bigotry and cultural stigmas during this period. Women's dilemmas and societal restrain became a vital subject for socially sensitive and liberal writers like Ismat Chughtai, Krishan Chander, Rajinder Singh Bedi and Ahmad Nadeem. Sadat Hasan Manto is also one of the writers who is remembered even today for his progressive works that dealt with the deplorable conditions of women during the twentieth century.

Sadat Hasan Manto belonged to the Progressive Writers Association. Literature belonging to the Progressive Writers Association talked about the necessity of the fundamental and societal revolution. Their primary focus was on the progression and liberation of women and their feelings. Sadat Hasan Manto, popularly known as Manto, wrote about this dilemma faced by women in an unhesitant manner.

When Manto began writing, he was regarded as a discordant writer of the time he belonged to. His stories, without any hesitation, threw light on the unusual shades of desires shared by males and females. Such topics were not taken up openly, and thus, Manto was looked down on for his writing style, which was trying to show a mirror to society. He was writing about incidents in society, the hypocrisy that existed in those times, and the discriminatory attitudes. These topics stirred an uproar in the stagnant setting that was least bothered. This paper has attempted to critically analyse a short story, *Hatak*, written by Manto, that discusses the two facades of society and how women were considered mere objects.

Of Wounded Souls – *Hatak*

'*Hatak*' or 'The Insult' is a true feminist short story written by Manto. The story's setting is in the times when India was struggling for Independence. It revolves around the life of a prostitute named Saugandhi. Manto's words in describing her make the reader realise that she is too emotional to be a prostitute. She is hard working and has a friendly relationship with her pimp Ram Lal. She is a quiet and kind woman and has the problem of getting too attached to her regular customers. This sweet lady cannot control her emotions when someone offers her love as at the end of the day, she is just a prostitute working in Mumbai. The story's climax comes when she decides to end her relationship with those men who made fake declarations of love. She comes face to face with the fact that all the men she had ever known have just used her. She recognised their sham feelings that were just present to use her caring heart and good nature. Consequently, she decides to toss them out of her life, literally and metaphorically.

Manto's *Hatak* is a true reflection of Mumbai's prostitutes during the Independence era. He devoted several stories to the prostitution business and very efficiently depicted that prostitutes are real women with real feelings just like any ordinary woman. Through stories like *Hatak*, Manto has emerged as a prominent figure who is all in for women's emancipation and feminism as a movement in literature.

The title of the story is decided upon the rejection of Saugandhi by a rich Seth. This wealthy man wanted to fulfill his physical desires. Though Saugandhi was tired after a long, uneasy day, she agrees to meet the rich man late at night in his car. It happens that when she arrives in front of Seth's car window, he throws a flashlight to have a look at Saugandhi. After taking a good look at her, he rejects her with the exclamation of 'ugh.' Without a word, Seth drives away immediately, indicating utter disgust. This incident fired up Saugandhi concerning the fact that someone, for the very first time, rejected her. She came face to face with certain realities: all the men she was in a relationship with were using her for sex and money; Madhu, the police sergeant who had expressed his desire to make her his wife one day, was just playing around to extract money from her. Though she was beautiful, Seth's 'ugh' made her realise that something extremely disgusting about her made Seth react in this manner, who had woken her up for his benefit. She realised that she was not more than an object to people like the rich Seth and police sergeant Madhu. These men who had prominent personalities in front of the whole world would secretly visit prostitutes like Saugandhi to satisfy their physical needs and discard them after. Saugandhi was pinched by Seth's arrogance. This incident led to an onset of a cycle of anger, and ultimately, she slept with her eczematous pet dog.

The rejection and the insult aflame several pent-up emotions within Saugandhi, which she finally vents out in front of Madhu. Seth's rejection made her realise the falsity of the men's promises to her. While reading the story, we can conclude that Saugandhi lived in a pitiful condition because she ultimately shared her room with an eczematous dog. She indeed admired herself and her physical features, but the text of the story throws light on the fact that she had a slimy, dirty pot to drink water from, which was rarely washed; that she had disheveled hair; that she wore dirty rags and she needed washing and cleaning. These deplorable conditions reflect her extremely poor situation. The reason for her poverty was Madhu who used to extract away all her hard-earned money in return for fake promises. This griminess is suggestive of the dire conditions in which many prostitutes of Mumbai lived in the Independence era.

According to Manto, living such a sad and unhygienic life in subhuman conditions is pitiable. Manto has reflected on the feminist theme regarding Saugandhi's liberation in this short story. The story is about Saugandhi's emancipation from the fake love bonds with men who did not love her, care for her, or respect her feelings as a human being. Their deceitful promises boiled her blood, and she flung them out of her life for once and for all. These men were not letting her be her true self.

Along with several other stories, this is one of Manto's stories that accurately depicts a prostitute's true living conditions. Manto describes Saugandhi's scanty belongings in her hut; the parrot in the birdcage with some food and moths flying over them; the description of Saugandhi's ill dog; her mucky sandals lying under the bed; the corner where she placed Lord Ganesha and the photos of her four clients; this entire narrative weaves the accurate picture of Saugandhi's life. The description transfers the readers into her world so that all the senses are deeply involved, and the readers get to experience the true essence of a prostitute's life.

Saugandhi's pimp, Ram Lal, is portrayed as a callous comedian. He is agitated because of the Prohibition Act regarding alcohol. He is not at all humorous, and a few incidents in the story highlight that he respects Saugandhi. He is aware that Saugandhi is spending her hard-earned money on Madhu, so he advises her to hide her money and lie about her income. This also brings to light the true nature of a Ram Lal. Though he is a pimp, he is the only human in Saugandhi's life who thinks about her well-being. He is the only kind individual in Saugandhi's life who treats her as a real human being. He comes to know about Saugandhi's real feelings towards Madhu but does not mock her love. In fact, in a concerned tone, he questions the sensibleness of her feelings. He seems to be the only voice of reason in the story while giving helpful advice to Saugandhi. He makes sure that he doesn't interfere in her personal matters like Madhu, who constantly belittles her on hygiene and home décor. Somewhere deep down in the heart Ram Lal is a good man concerned about his prostitutes and wants them to earn a decent amount. The readers can notice how patiently he waited at Saugandhi's door to meet Seth at night. He waited for almost an hour but did not abuse Saugandhi for making him wait. When Seth rejected Saugandhi, Ram Lal did not degrade Saugandhi. He took the rejection quite casually and went off to mind his own business. This is not the case with Saugandhi;

rejections are not a regular part of her work. But because of her disbelief regarding her self-worth, she took 'The Insult' too seriously. Though this insult rang a bell in her mind and gave her a reality check about the love with a man like Madhu. It knocked out the nonsense feeling of relationships and love cluttered in her mind.

Manto has this magic in his writing where the reader comes to understand the true personality of the characters. It is because of the minute details included in the story that we get to understand Saugandhi's nature. She is the one in the story who needs a counselor who can guide her with some good advice, but at the same time, she advises other young prostitutes about the prostitution business. She warns the young prostitutes about the quiet and young men. Therefore, it seems she has a good interpretation of human nature but fails to apply this understanding to practical use when it comes to her own life. This is a tragic truth of her life where she is always ready to help others but is unable to take a stand for herself. Saugandhi is Manto's most emotional character. A woman whose emotions always take a toll. The readers get to know the generous nature of this prostitute when they read the incident where she is ready to give the ticket price of a woman and her daughter though she is in a financial crunch. This throws light on the impracticality of Saugandhi, who herself is facing poor economic conditions but is ready to help others. This also shows her sympathetic nature towards others.

The feminist aspect of this story is the liberation of Saugandhi from barriers created by herself: her own emotions and sentiments about men. She attempts to unravel herself from the memories shared with those men by throwing their photographs. She disentangles her feelings towards them by tossing them out of the window. This sudden change is something not expected by Madhu, who tries to command her again. Madhu is astonished at the violence Saugandhi threw in his photograph, but he tries to control Saugandhi with his overpowering attitude. But Saugandhi, with a completely different personality, mocks and ridicules Madhu and even threatens to give a ring to the police. Dumbfounded, Madhu quickly disappears from Saugandhi's place.

When Madhu had come, he met a bonded woman in this kholi, but the caged woman was nowhere when he left. Now the home was resided by its valid owner: Saugandhi. We can notice a strange change in Saugandhi after this incident. We meet a peaceful Saugandhi who has cut all the ties with her male customers. We see a happy Saugandhi who picks her eczematous dog in her bed and doesn't hesitate to sleep beside him. This dog is the accurate portrayal of Saugandhi's newly formed character – sullied with dirt but full of pride. Another change that the insult brings in Saugandhi's nature is that she thinks she was rejected by Seth when she was perfect, so why not get dirty by sleeping next to a diseased dog. This also reflects that because of the insult, Saugandhi turned a bit deranged and had no problem with a highly tormented dog suffering from eczema. Manto is trying to draw parallels between the diseased dog and the rejected prostitute Saugandhi. The dog is sick and sullied, just like Saugandhi's soul and womanhood. But in the end, she decided to embrace her femininity, portrayed in the action of sleeping with this dirty, fur-losing dog. Somewhere the dog has a higher position in Saugandhi's life. It has never used Saugandhi or her money like the men in the photographs. Saugandhi was a compassionate and kindhearted woman who gave place to this dog in her house as she gave to the men in frames in her heart. The dog did not want anything in return like the men. Unlike the greedy men who wanted money or physical pleasures, the dog just wanted some affection. We meet the dog at a time when Saugandhi needs a protector. We see the dog barking at Madhu when she orders him to leave the kholi. This is the time when this diseased dog acts like an actual bodyguard. Saugandhi wanted his love and affection, who used to hide in her chest like a little baby, finally realised that happiness and satisfaction rely on a person's attitude towards life. It does not depend on another individual. Earlier, Saugandhi was looking for joy and love and believed that someone else would come and offer her this love unconditionally. But now, her search came to an end when she realised that she was responsible for her happiness. This self-emancipation was the real self-love she needed. Liberation from lies, betrayals and deceit was what Saugandhi required and achieved.

> "This roused Saugandhi. She found herself surrounded by a terrifying silence. Never before had she experienced this sort of dead stillness in her room. Everything seemed to be empty, like a train that has been shunted into a shed after all its passengers have alighted. She had an uneasy feeling that there was a sort of vacuum sucking at her from within. She tried her best to fill this void somehow but failed. She would crowd a number of thoughts in her head, but her mind was like a sieve. It remained empty.
>
> For a long time, Saugandhi sat in the cane chair and could think of no way of distracting herself. Suddenly, she picked up her dog and lying

> down in her spacious bed, went to sleep, with the mange-stricken animal in her arms (Manto 2007)."

Saugandhi's character has the objective and insight to realise her misuse. This unique characteristic helps her rise as a focused woman who decides to end the exploitation and finally set free from suppression. This is indeed an important reason why Manto's work was criticized by conservative dogmatists who were not familiar with such provocative and barefaced representation of women.

In the story mentioned above, *Hatak*, Manto explores the deception of civilisation and how a male-dominated society treats a female. Several times he underwent public expulsion and faced legal actions for being an actual speaker of social issues in the form of literary expression.

Conclusion

Manto's stories reinstated the long-drawn-out patriarchal beliefs of crudity and taboo incorporated with utmost humanism. In an insightful Urdu essay, *Manto, Aurat Aur Waris Alvi*, Najma Manzoor enunciates that:

> "Manto's aristocracy is such that he never preaches but continues to enlighten reader's minds and stir their conscience. Women have been subject to humiliation and Manto through his stories has empathized with their plight and has shown solidarity with their cause. His portrayals of domesticated women and prostitutes are unique for the associates unconventional attributes for example determination, will, not being content in every situation and above all the ability to laugh (Manzoor 2006)."

Being an insightful writer, Manto was highly disturbed by the political disorder. His tales address the idea of humanitarianism in a period when the nation was no less than a torrid bin of religious conflicts where misogynistic activities were performed in daylight in the name of communal dignity and nationalism. Manto construed his characters in a manner where they became symbols that drew attention to the extensive abuse faced by the human race in that period.

Manto was barely recognised and sourly accepted by a society that celebrated orthodoxy. Being a non-conformist, Manto was known as a rebellious intellectual through his literary texts. He wrote in the era when society wanted writers to imitate its traditions and not speak a word against the pricking conformism in their works.

However, Manto did not belong to the league of writers who emulated the practices set by the social order in their work. Manto was not ready to present a fabricated version of society; therefore, he wrote natural stories with meaningful insight. Even though he was accused of obscenity several times in his writing career, he kept writing stories that reflected his fundamental thoughts. While writing about Manto, Khalid Hasan stated that "how he could disrobe a society that was already naked. He did not beautify what was ugly nor hide what he felt should be exposed".

Manto is regarded as an essential writer for integrating the sexual ring in his work with remarkable honesty and candidness. His work reflects a distinguished form of suffering and trauma. His short story *Hatak* highlights the psychological strain that existed at that meantime. Accordingly, Manto soon was recognised as one of the most controversial Urdu writers of that era. He received a tremendous amount of admiration and praise from the readers for bringing to the surface both obvious and obscure tragedies in the Indian subcontinent.

Manto's female protagonists are strong and stubborn, unlike those usually in Urdu narratives. Urdu narratives written in those times had the approach of presenting women as vaguely debased characters and underlined merely the prevalent traditions of cultures. Undoubtedly, Manto dared to grant a fiery tongue to beings' opinions, like prostitutes, that were bullied in society and considered browbeaten. He wanted to declare their independence in the double-façade society. The diversity in his characters shocked the readers, and his work's directness resulted in his exclusion from society. Still, he did not hesitate to produce work with characters ready to break the shackles and wanted to come out of the closet. Sadat Hasan Manto, as a writer, was one of a kind who was prepared to cross the set boundaries and explore fields that were considered shameful to talk or write about.

Works Cited

Das, Veena. "Language and body: Transactions in the construction of pain". *Daedalus* 125.1, 1996, 67-91.

Das, Veena; Nandy, Ashis. "Violence, victimhood, and the language of silence." *Contributions to Indian Sociology* 19.1, 1985, 177-95.

Das, Veena; Singh, Bhrigupati. *Critical Events: An Anthropological Perspective on Contemporary India*. Oxford University Press: Delhi. 1995.

Gopal, Priyamvada. *Literary Radicalism in India: Gender, nation and the transition to independence*. Routledge, 2012.

Jalal, Ayesha. "Secularists, subalterns and the stigma of 'communalism': Partition historiography revisited". *Modern Asian Studies* 30. 3, 1996, 681-737.

Manto, Saadat Hasan. *For Freedom's Sake: Selected Stories and Sketches*, trans. and ed. Mohammad Asaduddin, Karachi: Oxford University Press, 2001, 131-4.

Manto, Saadat Hasan. *Selected Stories* Translated from Urdu with an Introduction by Khalid Hasan. New Delhi, India: Penguin, 2007.

Manzoor, Najma. 'Manto, Aurat Aur Waris Alvi'. In Fahmida Riaz (Ed.), *Adab ki Nisai Rad-eTashkeel*. Karachi: Wada Kitab Ghar, 2006.

Rumi, Ahmad, Raza. "Reclaiming Humanity: Women in Manto's Short Stories". *Social Scientist*. 2012, 75-86.

Saeed, Saadia. "Manto and Women". *The Nation*. Nawai Waqt Group. 2018. https://nation.com.pk/01-Dec-2018/manto-and-women

https://www.insaneowl.com/the-insult-or-hatak-by-saadat-hasan-manto-short-story-analysis/

CHAPTER 9

Women Psychology

Dr. Smritikana Ghosh

The psychology of females addresses the social, economic, and political concerns that women face throughout their lives. Gender and female human identity difficulties, as well as the challenges that women experience throughout their lives, are addressed in women's psychology. For those interested in the psychology of women, critical analysis of all subfields of psychology is encouraged. Studies in the field of women's psychology explore issues such as gender stereotyping; physical development in female life cycles; theoretical perspectives on the personalities and mental well-being of females; sexuality; reproductive rights; nonverbal and verbal communication by and about females; female intimacy and romantic relationships; women's career psychology; female leadership; female power; violence against females; and many more.

Through empirical research in the area of women's psychology, a wide range of subjects are addressed, including the integration of work and family life, day care, violence against women, child abductions, and missing children. There are those who call this field of research feminist psychology since it aims to understand the individual in relation to larger political and social contexts. Applied feminist psychoanalysis is a branch of psychology dedicated to studying and better understanding women. In both their psyche and genetics, men and women are vastly different from one another. When it comes to hormones, women and men are very different. In contrast to the testosterone-coated male brain, the female brain is overflowing with oestrogen and progesterone. In addition to making a woman more social, oestrogen enhances a woman's capability to empathise with and comprehend the emotions of others (Schulte-Ruther et al., 2008).

The Psychological Dilemma of the Indian Women

The housewife of the future is an ideal of Indian femininity in every way. Throughout her life, she has worked tirelessly to satisfy the needs of others and her own family. She is devoted to her job and thrives when her employers are successful. Indian housewives frequently present to their psychiatrists as patients with somatisation or conversion disorders, hoping that their family members will listen and assist them in their time of need.

Despite their so-called freedom, Indian women are still seen as second-class citizens in many parts of the country. For the most part, Indian families don't lament the birth of a female child. Girls who are born into a family are usually criticised by other family members and even referred to as a "curse" by some. Even her own parents, who live in a patriarchal world, humiliate and mistreat her. Despite her many accomplishments, she is still unable to win her parents' respect and affection, despite their adoration for her. In spite of her best efforts, she can't help but feel sad and hungry all the time.

Mental Health and Mental Disorder

The term "mental health" refers to a person's level of mental or emotional well-being or the absence of a mental disorder. Positivist or holistic approaches to mental health argue that a person's ability to enjoy life and maintain a healthy equilibrium between the various dimensions of their personhood and the efforts they make to improve their mental toughness is an important part of their overall well-being. It's also known as mental illness, a psychological or behavioural pattern that emerges without the individual's consent and is supposed to create mental or physical impairments that are not anticipated as part of normal growth or culture. People with mental health problems shouldn't be expected to have them as a normal part of their growth or culture.

A person's gender is one of the most significant aspects in determining their mental health and illness. Gender-specific characteristics and processes that promote and sustain mental health and resilience in the face of stress and adversity have received significantly less attention than the morbidity associated with mental disorders. People's gender is a major influence in determining their mental health and illness. Gender-specific characteristics and processes that promote and sustain mental health and resilience in the face of stress and adversity have received significantly less attention than the morbidity associated with mental disorders.

The patterns of psychiatric diseases and psychological distress reported in women vary from those observed in males, according to an analysis of mental health indices and data. Depression, anxiety, and other forms of psychological distress are twice as common in men as they are in women. However, men are more prone to suffering from substance abuse, mental health issues, and psychopathic traits.

Common Mental Disorders

According to the results of a new study, depression, anxiety, and other common mental disorders (CMDs) are more prevalent in women than in men. Unipolar depression is estimated to be the second leading cause of disability globally by 2020, with a prevalence rate of two times that of males. Females have a two to three times greater lifetime risk of developing diseases such as generalised anxiety disorder (Pigott, 2002).

Depression is not just the most common mental health problem for women, but it also has the potential to be more long-lasting in women than in men. Despite the fact that depression symptoms in men and women are frequently regarded to be equivalent in general, women are more likely to present with unexpected or "reverse vegetative" symptoms, including increased appetite and weight gain. More women than men have anxiety disorders, and their symptoms tend to be more pronounced and their recovery process more difficult to navigate.

Severe Mental Illness

Schizophrenia and bipolar illness are less common than CMD, but the chronic course and impairment associated with these diseases make them more severe. Not only do those who are afflicted by these diseases suffer greatly because of the stigma attached to them, but so do their loved ones. In many situations, families are left to care for the majority of these patients for the majority of their lives.

Schizophrenia and bipolar disorder, which affect 2% of the population, show no significant gender variations in prevalence (Piccinelli & Homen, 1997). Nevertheless, gender disparities have been shown in a variety of areas, including when symptoms first appear, clinical characteristics, the severity and duration of these diseases, social adjustment, and long-term outcomes. Female bipolar disorder sufferers had more bouts of depression and were more likely to have "rapid cycling" and a seasonal pattern in their moods (Freeman, Arnold, & McElroy, 2002). As shown by large cross-cultural research on the subject, psychosis in women has a better prognosis in emerging nations. In addition, girls are more likely to develop schizophrenia at a later age than boys.

Women's Collectives and Psychosocial Support

The introduction and implementation of a feminist intervention is no doubt a challenging task. Community-based women's collectives, which are supported by state and NGO programmes and which have evolved spontaneously to address gender-based violence, were found to be safe places for women to voice concerns. The collectives have emerged as a critical forum for victims of domestic violence to raise awareness of the issue and connect them to relevant services, such as counselling, mediation, and other kinds of alternative dispute resolution based on human rights principles (ICRW, 2018; Nair, 2020). In South India, a community-based movement was started in 2000 to address the interrelated problems of poverty and gender inequity. In terms of its size, it's the most significant in the continent's whole region (Vindhya et al., 2018; Vindhya & Lingam, 2019). For this initiative, establishing women's self-help groups with the purpose of generating money via micro-credit was essential. Aside from microcredit, the intervention delivered social empowerment via collectively driven methods to address gender-based violence as well as economic empowerment. This intervention was made possible by the construction of community-managed family counselling centres that served as resources for victims of domestic violence in need of counselling, mediation, and conflict resolution, even if the details aren't relevant to the present topic.

For victims and perpetrators alike, establishing a network of local psychological services makes it easier to create rapport and trust. This system's key strength was connecting survivors with institutional assistance. Vindhya and Lingam (2019) describe the complete support system, including the delivery of services, as centred on the woman's expectations and needs. This intervention "may be deemed to resonate with a feminist worldview and is survivor-focused." While the technique stresses "women's interests first," the focus on validation of women's experiences, and the identification of violence as unacceptable, the paradox is that it seems to support conventional male-centric gender norms and the demand that women "adapt" as required. Even though these services are sometimes called "counseling," they are really a native and culturally-based form of mental health help that includes patient listening, funny arguments from the elderly, and veiled warnings to stop being violent. As a result of the collectives' long-term success, their legal counsel is more likely to follow through on their promises (Vindhya & Lingam, 2019). A culturally ingrained feminist perspective, whatever its imperfections, is what leads and motivates state and non-government initiatives to prevent violence against women. This is what women's organisations are doing.

Identities and Reaffirmation of Gender Stereotypes

For decades, researchers have looked at how the state shapes women's political and economic identities (Sonpar & Kapur, 2001). Some feminist experts have noticed that the Indian government has had a range of viewpoints on this matter. State-sponsored programmes are part of the government's larger development policy, which aims to empower women economically and give them more control over their lives. Women's empowerment programmes, according to Calman (1992) and Sen and Batliwala (2000), use the term "empowerment," which implies a sense of self-assuredness, assertiveness, and the capacity to confront unfair power imbalances as well as get through difficult social circumstances.

Psychosocial Aspects of Women's Reproductive Health

During pregnancy and childbirth

About one-third of all pregnant or menstruating women suffer from the above-mentioned condition of poor mental health. 80% of women, especially those who have been abused, are apprehensive about their pregnancy and the hardships of delivery. A healthy pregnancy and delivery are hindered by concerns about the health of the mother and child; pain during labour; delivery technique; the future role of life; family response to a female kid or an unwanted baby; and pregnancy problems like caesarean section or assisted birth. In India, the problem may be made worse by a lack of support, autonomy in making decisions, limited prenatal care, a desire for a boy, and a lack of counselling and perinatal mental health therapies.

Influence on fertility

It is possible to exert some degree of control over one's own fertility by making lifestyle choices such as where one chooses to live (urban or rural), who one knows personally (such as spouses), and what one believes (Standley, 1994). In India, the most influential person in decision-making is the husband, who is often swayed by his family (Sarder et al., 2021). Because of social and cultural norms, women are compelled to have a family as soon as they are married. A woman's mental health may suffer if she is unable to conceive. Many women suffer from this illness, which is typically linked to marital difficulties and domestic abuse, as well as a decrease in sexual closeness and the desire for mental recovery (Jisha & Thomas, 2017).

Pregnancy loss

Every 1,000 women between the ages of 15 and 49 have an abortion (Singh et al., 2018). Artificially inducing miscarriage is more common in single women than in married people. Female foeticide may be predicted by a desire for a male kid, which is often influenced by societal norms. According to Kotta et al. (2018), approximately half of all women who have had a miscarriage suffer from post-traumatic stress disorder and depression. Despite the fact that many women who have had a miscarriage choose not to seek outside assistance, there aren't enough resources available to assist those who do.

Menopause

In women, the start of menopause is strongly linked to the development of mental health issues. Anger, anxiety, and depression are all-too-common mental health issues. Menopause may cause serious problems with sexual function. With menopause comes a loss of fertility, vitality, and attractiveness, as well as the belief that women are less desirable. When it comes to focusing on one's own life, now is the time. Most people don't seek out and accept psychological counselling as a normal part of their lives.

Gynecological Conditions

One in every three women in India suffers from some kind of dysmenorrhea. This may lead to symptoms including anxiety, impatience, difficulties concentrating; sleep deprivation, and forgetfulness, as well as stress and a decreased quality of life. Another prevalent gynecological condition, affecting as many as half of all women of reproductive age, is infection of the reproductive tract. In addition to melancholy, anxiety, somatoform illness, culture-bound syndrome, and sexual dysfunction, there are a number of other disorders that might accompany these symptoms. Low-income and less-educated people are more likely to have these symptoms.

Psychological Well-being of Indian Women

Personal self-esteem and the ability to carry out everyday tasks are both important aspects of a person's mental health. In this dynamic state, a person develops contentment and pleasure by finding a balance between the challenging and rewarding events in their life. It is a state of being. An individual's lifespan and quality of health are more likely to be extended when they have a strong mental health foundation. Those who remain at home to care for children are well-known to suffer from poor mental health. Stress may have a greater impact on those who have lower degrees of self-efficacy and self-acceptance (a good attitude about one's own life). Lack of knowledge and a lack of cultural and religious conservatism have been connected to low autonomy, which measures an individual's sense of self-determination and independence. Personal elements such as financial autonomy, the capacity to make choices, and the freedom to move around are all key components of the feeling of autonomy that people have. 57% of women, according to a government poll, do not have domestic autonomy or the flexibility to leave the home anytime they like. As an example, a study indicated that 35% of women lack the capacity to make their own financial choices, 62% lack the freedom to travel, and 72% lack control over their homes. It's not obvious whether the notion of life's (a feeling of meaning and purpose) will ever be realised or even recognised. Many people's primary focus in life is to become engaged in some area of the family life they lead, despite the fact that this tendency is evolving. People's socioeconomic level has an impact on the quality of their relationships, which may be characterised as amicable, enjoyable, and trustworthy interactions with others. When it comes to defining the kind of relationships that women may have, males are often given the most important role. Even now, interracial dating and marriages are frowned upon in India. About 41% of women have been victims of domestic violence, which shows that there aren't enough ways to socialise at home (Sengupta et al., 2017).

Burden of Care

Because of cultural norms and gendered expectations, women are more likely than males to assume the role of caregiver. Caretakers for the elderly make up between 57% and 81% of the workforce. Social and cultural conventions, as well as the fact that women are more likely to be jobless, account for this. Due to their many responsibilities, they face conflict in their jobs, strain in their duties, and overload in their roles. Due to role conflict and role strain, they were more likely to suffer from physical and mental health concerns. When caring for someone who has a common physical condition like cerebrovascular disease, Parkinson's disease, greater disability, urinary incontinence, or insomnia for an average of 38 hours per week, Brinda and colleagues found that approximately 10% of these women develop depression as a result of their caring obligations. They spend 15.2 hours a day taking care of their families and 8.4 hours on housekeeping, with rural women spending more time on housework than their urban counterparts (Sharma, Chakrabarti, & Grover, 2016).

Emerging Hopes

In 1951, just 8.9 percent of women had a high school diploma, but by 2004, that figure had risen to more than 57 percent. The obvious changes in social and economic position that education has brought about have resulted in a higher standard of living and psychological well-being for many people (Nair, 2010). Women's help-seeking behaviour is impacted by their education. Women's mental health awareness and treatment choices are projected to improve as society progresses in the twenty-first century. Women's rights are being bolstered through constitutional safeguards, government programmes that promote more women to work, and participation in national-building activities. The government has made no significant attempts to date to improve the mental health of women in society. A few recent innovations in the field are expected to have a positive impact on mental health care. As the number of people who work in mental health has gone up, the number of psychiatrists has gone down.

Women's mental health is one of the benefits of the district mental health programme, which has various perks. The introduction of psychiatry in the MBBS curriculum by the Indian Medical Council may help medical students better comprehend the difficulties surrounding women's mental health. This is the first time the Indian government has put up a national mental health strategy. Women's mental health is a developing issue in India, thus the country's psychiatric organisation organised a committee to address it. Several studies and writings published on social media have brought these concerns to the notice of Indian psychiatrists. Abuse of women has been related to mental illness, and many non-governmental organisations (NGOs) are attempting to put an end to it. There is some evidence that the public's increased understanding of mental illness, which is being disseminated via print and electronic media, is helping to reduce stigma. With the ease with which educated individuals may get information, the majority of material relevant to mental health is currently accessible via the media (Loganathan & Kreuter, 2014).

Conclusions

An enormous amount of emotional and social pressure is placed on women in India. Social value systems; culture; tradition; illiteracy; poverty; and so on all have a role in determining the majority of the weight. An individual's mental health may be affected by the burden of psychosocial variables. A multi-pronged approach is required to address this issue. Experts in mental health play a critical role in identifying and addressing the underlying psychological burden when addressing mental health concerns. The complexity of the responsibilities, the expectations, and the tensions of the positions has led to an increase in the proportion of women having mental health issues. Individuality is on the rise for these women, but their narrations suggest a feeling of guilt connected with having an entirely distinct identity; hence, they make sacrifices in order to fit in better with the rest of society. In light of the tremendous cultural transformations taking place in our country, we need to know more about the changing identities of Indian women. According to the conclusions of this research, men need to be educated about the changing requirements of women in their psychosocial environment and to regard them as beings that are not always "in relation" but rather as having an "independent identity." This should be done to help men become more aware of the issue. Women have a natural tendency to depend on others, which shows how hard it is for them to break away from traditional ideas about the roles they play in their psychological environment.

Work Cited

Calman, L. (1992). *Toward empowerment: Women and movement politics in India.* Boulder, CO: Westview Press.

Freeman, M.P, Arnold, L.M, & McElroy, S.L. (2002). "Bipolar disorder." In: Kornstein SG, Clayton AH, editors. *Women's Mental Health & – A Comprehensive Textbook.* New York: The Gulliford Press, 166–81.

International Center for Research on Women (2018). *Role of women's collectives in addressing intimate partner violence in India: A policy brief.* New Delhi, India: ICRW.

Jisha, P.R, & Thomas, I. (2017). "Psychological aspects in infertility: A comparative study." *IOSR J Humanit Soc Sci*; 22:88-95.

Kotta, S., Molangur, U., Bipeta, R., & Ganesh, R. (2018). "A cross-sectional study of the psychosocial problems following abortion." *Indian J Psychiatry*; 60:217-23.

Loganathan, S & Kreuter, M. (2014). "Audience segmentation: Identifying key stakeholders for mental health literacy interventions in India." *J Public Ment Health*; 13:159-70.

Nair, N. (2010). "Women's education in India: A situational analysis." *IMJ;* 1:100-14

Piccinelli, M. & Homen, F., (1997). *Gender Differences in the Epidemiology of Affective Disorders and Schizophrenia.* Geneva: World Health Organisation.

Pigott T.A. (2002). "Women's Mental Health – A Comprehensive Textbook." In: *Kornstein SG,* Clayton AH, editors. The Gulliford Press: New York;. 195–22.

Rondung, E., Thomten., J, & Sundin, O. (2016). "Psychological perspectives on fear of childbirth." *J Anxiety Disord*, 44:80-91.

Sarder, A, Islam, S.M, Maniruzzaman, Talukder, A, & Ahammed B. (2021). *Prevalence of unintended pregnancy and its associated factors: Evidence from six south Asian countries.* PLoS One; 16:e0245923

Schulte-Ruther M, Markowitsch, H.J, Shah, N.J, Fink, & G.R, Piefke, M. (2008). "Gender differences in brain networks supporting empathy." *Neuroimage.* 42:393–403.

Sen, G., & Batliwala. S. (2000). "Empowering women for reproductive rights." In H. B. Presser & G. Sen (Eds.), *Women's empowerment and demographic processes* (14–28). New York, NY: Oxford University Press.

Sengupta, S., Sachdeva, S., Chigateri, S., Zaidi, M., & Chopra, D. (2017). From Double Burden of Women to a "Double Boon": Balancing Unpaid Care Work and Paid Work. Policy Brief. Brighton, England: Institute of Development Studies.

Sharma N, Chakrabarti S, Grover S. (2016). "Gender differences in caregiving among family – caregivers of people with mental illnesses." *World J Psychiatry*; 6:7-17.

Singh, S., Shekhar, C., Acharya, R., Moore, A.M, Stillman, M, & Pradhan, M.R, (2018). "The incidence of abortion and unintended pregnancy in India, 2015." *Lancet Glob Health*; 6:e111-20.

Sonpar, S., & Kapur, R. (2001). "Non-conventional indicators: Gender disparities under structural reforms." *Economic and Political Weekly*, 6–12.

Standley, T. (1984). "Psychosocial aspects of fertility control." In: Harrison RF, Bonnar J, Thompson W, editors. *Fertility and Sterility*. Dordrecht: Springer.

Vindhya, U., & Lingam, L. (2019). "Social action committees: Community intervention to reduce gender-based violence." *Indian Journal of Gender Studies*, 26(3), 263–287.

Vindhya, U., Kashyap, A., Bhatla, N., Nandi, S., & Pal, P. (2018). "Velugu/Indira Kranti Patham – Society for elimination of rural poverty: A model documentation report on addressing intimate partner violence in India." New Delhi, *India: International Center for Research on Women*.

CHAPTER 10

Women amidst the Mayhem of Partition

Shrishti Dey

Abstract

The partition of 1947 was not just a physiological or geographical aberration in the autobiographical history of the nation. What also pervaded the undercurrent of this partition is a glitch in the collective and individual cultural memory of the masses. This collision led to the crumbling of identity and the organic creation of a traumatic space. This infertile space of cultural trauma and fractured identity houses the memories of men, women and children. This chapter shall elaborate on the experiences and traumatic backdrops of women caught in this whirlwind of nation vs. community. The chapter aims to analyse the question of partition trauma through the lens of women's identity.

Keywords: Partition, Trauma, Family, Home, Border

Introduction

The celebration of the decolonisation of British rule in India was an expensive prize paid for by the division of the colony into two sovereign states. The process of partition carried in its body a plethora of violence, mass killings, torture and damage. The abstract notion of a boundary had great historic repercussions. This division of the nation-state into two and then later three states marked the transfer of power from the British nationalists to the rulers of each state. After partition, the nation's came to be seen as open wounds. The people, who inhabited these countries, had the trauma embedded into their psychological framework.

The partition and the stir that followed have taken citizens into an everlasting loop of historical trauma and botched-up collective memory. The chapter attempts to delineate the experience of violence, trauma and displacement that is synonymous with the lives of subjects of the post-colonial states. These individual countries that were promised a new dawn of freedom often find themselves journeying through a tunnel of confusion and homesickness, a desire to be with their own people. Through the texts this chapter shall analyse the gendered violence and trauma that dwells in the waters of partition.

Women are always seen as a liability in times of crisis. This chapter will take in its ambit the story of women who suffer a dual tragedy brought about by their gender and the partition. Such narratives allow filling the gaps left by the male narratives of partition trauma. The two texts that have been elaborated below are – *The Shadow Lines* and *Ice-Candy-Man.*

Freud in his *Beyond the Pleasure Principle* talks about the development of hysteria or hypochondria that arises out of a mechanical shock. He also labeled it as "traumatic neurosis." This mechanical shock came as a form of partition and war in the texts discussed in this chapter. Under the medical gaze, this trauma is expressed through the symptoms of psychological in equilibrium, lack of control, connection and meaning in the individual.

Amitav Ghosh's *The Shadow Lines* is a diligent enterprise to voice personal narratives embedded into the framework of public tragedy. The novel, led by the narrator's journey towards unearthing old connections, brings to the forefront repressed experiences that have catapulted trauma to the surface. It is the character of Thamma, who acts out as Ghosh's mouthpiece to embody the crushing spirit of partition and the following trauma. She is the victim and witness to the 1964 riots between West Bengal and Bangladesh that resonated with the partition of India and Pakistan. Thamma is born in Dhaka but migrates to Calcutta as a result of the partition. She thereby leads a life of desiring reconciliation with her older self and older identity. She struggles to reunite with the land where she was born. It is upon paying a visit to Bangladesh that she realises it has now become a foreign entity. Going closer to her home only brings upon her the tragic realisation that home has gone farther away from her.

Her identity as an Indian robbed her off the identity that she was born with, the one she resonated with. The partition was accompanied by loots, rapes and killings, all sugarcoated with the dream of freedom. In a single night, the identities of these women were changed. These imaginary lines drawn between the two nations caught in its throes women like Thamma who live a life cursed by the memories of a long lost land. This freedom brought separation anxiety and depression to Thamma, who left a part of her own family back in Bangladesh. She is treated as an outsider in the courtyard of her own home. The gift of a new nation fills Thamma with the perennial longing for home and happiness. As Suvir Kaul asserts "A growing sense that the logic of the nation-state is necessarily at odds with various forms of sub-continental community – that to be Indian is to be perversely and perhaps unsuccessfully define oneself against one's mirror image from across the border." – the concept of nation and home are mutually exclusive for Thamma who has borne the brunt of partition.

Ghosh has portrayed Thamma as the onus of change in the novel. As a history graduate from Dhaka University, it was an ardent desire for freedom that burned inside of her. She also desired to help a terrorist in her class just to embrace freedom. "I would have killed him. It was for our freedom: I would have done anything to be free." Her notion of nationalism was colored by the impression cast upon her by the freedom fighters of Bengal. She romanticised the idea of freedom and was ignorant of the severe repercussions of this desire for freedom. Thamma suffers the crisis of dual identity like diasporic people. The Bengali lingual tendency to say I am coming instead of I am going finds voice in Thamma's confusion. She is at crossroads. She is unaware of whether she is going away or coming home.

This eagerness for freedom coupled with a nationalistic spirit is challenged by her homesickness for Bangladesh once she started growing old in India. It is her quest for a solid national identity that made her oppose Ila's decision to stay in England. She finds it difficult to accept that there can be a border separating her own family members and assign a different identity to them. Before visiting Dhaka, she asks her son about the absence of bold border lines – "if there's no difference, both sides will be the same; it'll be just like it used to be before, when we used to catch a train in Dhaka and get off in Calcutta the next day without anybody stopping us." She thus, finds all the war and the killing futile as there is no concrete boundary between the two nations that is visible from the airplane- "What was it all for then – partition and all the killing and everything – if there isn't something in between"

There is a constant tussle that we see in her character. She dwells in the sweet yet long lost memory of her childhood home in Dhaka, while walking the corridors of her new home in Calcutta. The past that she so desperately wished to forget interferes in her present way of life. It is this continous string of memories that she wishes to answer by travelling to Dhaka. In her old childhood home, she gets nostalgic about her childhood, the balconies that she and Mayadebi would play in and the terrace. These memories hold no value among the refugees who now inhabit that home. Thus, this childhood and its associated memories only herald pain and suffering for Thamma.

As a young woman in Dhaka, the spirit of nationalism burnt inside of her. She wished to participate in the movement for chasing the British out of India. Long after the separation of India and Bangladesh and the death of two family members, she realises that her gift of freedom stood strong upon the sacrificial alter of her own family. The citizens of Bangladesh are now the 'Other' to her. The binary is more stark and compelling as it is her own family across the border that refuses to accept her.

Ghosh creates a sense of déjà vue through the character of Thamma. She recalls how their ancestral home in Dhaka had a wooden partition separating her family and her Jethamoshai's. They lived as separate families under the same roof. When she goes to visit him, years later, it is the same hatred that greets her. There is a deep rooted contempt in the way Thamma's Jethamoshai talks of her family-" "they [his brother and sister in law] had two daughters: one with a face like a vulture, and another one who was as poisonous as a cobra."

The desire to revisit Dhaka remains dormant in her throughout her service life. It is only after retirement that the memory of her Dhaka home and her Jethamoshai comes crawling to her. She desires to go back to her home. After the bitter rendezvous with her Jethamoshai in Dhaka and Tridib's tragic death, she realises that she has no 'home'. The imaginary lines created between the two countries and also the ones drawn in their psyche, is indispensible. The trauma caused by this separation and the disrupted memory is a collective experience. Thamma realises that though the food, language, culture of the people on both sides of the border is same; there is always a separate reality that exists on the other side.

It is Tridib's death that jerks Thamma out of her emotional coma. She learns that Bangladesh is no more her own. She wished for the freedom of her nation but was treated as an outcast upon her arrival. Her past was painted by the memory of her being a young girl, fighting for East Bengal. Her present is pained by the realisation that it is because of her visit to her homeland that Tridib was killed. The romanticised notion of freedom that she once housed, is annihilated by this incident and she attaches the feeling of hatred to the people in Bangladesh who were once her own. Communal feelings intervened with the feeling of brotherhood and oneness that Thamma hoped to find. Eventually, she gets easy with the idea of borders and the sense of alienation from the people of Bangladesh. This acceptance is rooted in a sense of trauma. According to Freud "the individual has little control over the contents of the unconscious, and uses defense mechanisms to deal with information contained therein." She uses hatred to get over her painful nostalgia of Dhaka and her estranged family.

Ice-candy – man by Bapsi Sidhwa is a seminal text in the chronology of studying partition trauma through the eyes of women. Written by a Pakistani author, with a Parsi girl Lenny as its narrative vehicle, this work elaborates on the repercussions of Partition and its tremors felt in Lahore, Pakistan. Lenny is a constant companion to her Ayah, Shanta, whose body represents the violence and torture that partition is synonymous with. Women's bodies, in the context of partition, become the site of claiming or safeguarding honour. Her body suffers a juxtaposition of interests-one that would snatch her virtue to satisfy communal hatred and the other that would choose death for her to chastise her.

She is desired strongly by her endless string of admirers. Ayah's bevy of friends includes people across communities. This inter-community friendship represents the very sentiment of Pre partitioning India. She reserves the choice of men to herself. Ayah's character sketch starts off as a challenge to the male-dominated society that easily commoditised women. She is aware of her sexuality. She didn't fear enveloping her curves under the veil of modesty. This sets her as an antithesis to the male gaze prevalent in pre-partition India.

Lenny, growing up in Lahore during the tumultuous time of partition comes to realise that the sexual humiliation that Ayah suffers is a physical and more obvious manifestation of the violence meted out to women under the radar of partition. Shanta is abducted, raped and forced into a marriage by one of her admirers, the ice-candy man. This is understood as her punishment for her flamboyance that threatened the masculine tyranny of her times. Her indirect refusal to conform to the societal notions of femininity and chastity brought her doom in the form of physical and emotional abuse, facilitated by the ice candy man. She is sold off as a courtesan, by her most eligible suitor, the ice candy man. She is then set up at Hira Mandi, widely known for its notoriety. Her accommodation at Hira Mandi as a prostitute earns her an identity of bad repute and leaves her traumatised. These changes flooding the life of Shanta are a representation of the violence and transformation that is associated with the partition. Both Shanta and Hamida are mere puppets in the hands of male authority, which turned a blind eye to their individual identities and used them as per their convenience.

In Lenny's broken description of the events that she witnesses, there is evidence of aporia or destruction of language. According to Elaine in her book *The Body in Pain –The Making and Unmaking of the World,* reversion to the language of cries and groans, and everything incomprehensible, is often rooted in events that are coloured with trauma. This novel is a figment of her reality that was shrouded by the horrors of ethnic genocide. She once asserted "My intention was to write about Partition because very little had been written about it. There are certain images from my past which have always haunted me … Although I was very young then, I saw chance killings, fires, and dead bodies. These are images which have stayed with me … This hostility needs to be dealt with.

Lenny's voice as the narrator is the meeting ground of a multitude of voices from the periphery of the social circle. She belongs to a lesser-known community of the Parsis and is polio-stricken. It is her own marginalisation that finds voice alongside all the women who are sidelined by men occupying the crux of the society. The novel depicts the violence-laden birth of Pakistan through the muted narratives of women. Through the agency of narration at her disposal, Lenny fills the gaps in the collage of male-centric narratives of the partition.

The novel traces her transition from being a sexually independent woman in the pre-partition era to being a sexual commodity under the male gaze in post-partition India. Talking of women caught up in the turmoil of partition, Sidhwa writes "metamorphosis of women into possessions; living objects on whose soft bodies' victors and losers alike vent their wrath, enact fantastic vendettas, celebrate victories." Ayah was constantly pulled by two opposing forces, much like two opposing sides during a partition. Her identity was reduced to the rope in a tug of war on one side was the man she loved, the masseur, and on the other was the ice candy man. Her horrific abduction, an activity carried out to mark her body as the man's territory is described as follows "The last thing I noticed was Ayah, her mouth slack and piteously gaping, her disheveled hair flying into her kidnappers' faces, staring at us as if she wanted to leave behind her wide-open and terrified eyes."

The abduction of Ayah comes as a shock to Lenny, who was otherwise well versed with the camaraderie that Shanta shared with her male friends and admirers. The transition from a well-connected secular group to a group of rivals separated by the partition and the resultant communal distance was well witnessed by eight-year-old Lenny. She writes "And I become aware of religious differences. It is sudden. One day everybody is themselves – and the next day they are Hindu, Muslim, Sikh, Christian. People shrink, dwindling into symbols." It is sheer communal hatred and jealousy that instigates the Ice candy man to berate the woman he loved and kill her beloved. She comes to be seen as a prize, taken home by the one who emerges victorious in the communal warfare. The envy expressed by Ice candy man meets its fate when the mutilated body of the Masseur is found.

Ayah's image of an object of desire transforms into that of a Hindu woman whose virtue needs to be violated to exact revenge. Ice-candy man abducts her with a host of his Muslim followers and sells her off as a prostitute. This reduction and humiliation of identity is the trigger for trauma that haunts Ayah for the rest of her life.

As a 'fallen woman,' Ayah is advised not to go back to her family as they would not accept her. However; Ayah considers her abduction and multiple rapes to be an event more traumatic than anything else. The horror of the event casts a deep scar on her psyche. Lenny notes her "vacant eyes are bigger than ever: wide-opened with what they've seen and felt." Long after being rescued from the clutches of the Ice candy man, the trauma lingers on in her memory and becomes a part of her history. Her trauma is the representation of the psychological aberration that inhabits the life of most women during and after the partition. Her abduction, rape, marriage to the man who wronged her and conversion to Mumtaz – all bear testimony to how women were seen as the baton of settlement, to mask the horrors of partition.

Ayah tells Lenny's godmother that she has relatives in Amritsar that she can go back to. There is no mention of home. For a woman who has stepped out of her home in the pre-partition era, only to be abducted and raped later in Lahore, home does become an alien entity. Her desperation to go back to her roots, to Amritsar, despite the possibility of non-acceptance, depicts that she no longer feels safe and comfortable in Lahore. The novel ends with an image of Ayah crossing the Wagah border. It is unknown whether she finds home, acceptance and closure, just like the aftermath of many wronged women who have crossed borders.

Conclusion

Both Thamma and Ayah are located at sites of partition. Thamma becomes a foreigner in her own land and Ayah is wronged by the ones who claimed to love and admire her. Both stories trace the trajectory of how there is a lingering lack of closure that follows these two individuals everywhere. The trauma that they face is rooted in emotional abuse and sexual abuse respectively, however; a common sense of dejection and betrayal by family and friends accompanies their difficulty to move forward in life.

Works Cited

Ghosh, Amitav. *The Shadow Lines*. New Delhi: Oxford University Press, 1995. Print

Sidhwa, Bapsi. *Ice-Candy-Man*. London: Penguin, 1989. Print

Caruth, Cathy. *Unclaimed Experience: Trauma, Narrative, and History*. Maryland: The Johns Hopkins University Press Ltd, 1996. Print

Yadav, Akhil. "Re-defining Socio-Political Identities in Amitav Ghosh's The Shadow Lines." *Indian Scholar*. Vol.3, no. 4, 2017, pp.348-351

Mansoor, Asma. "Ice Candy Man." *The Literary Encyclopaedia*. 2020

Scarry, Elaine. *The Body in Pain –The Making and Unmaking of the World*. New York: Oxford University Press. 1985. Print

Choudhury, Jharna. "Study of Trauma and Transgression of the 'Adult-child' in Bapsi Sidhwa's Ice-Candy-Man."*Rupkatha Journal on Interdisciplinary Studies in Humanities*. vol. 12, no. 5. 2020. pp. 1-5

Mohanram, Radhika. "Trauma, cultural memory and the Indian partition." *Cultural studies*. Vol.25, no. 6, 2011, pp. 917-934

Roy, Rituparna." 2 Women during the Partition: Victim and agent." *South Asian Partition Fiction in English: From Khushwant Singh to Amitav Ghosh*, Amsterdam University, pp. 63-88

Black, Shameem. "Cosmopolitanism at Home: Amitav Ghosh's The Shadow Lines." *The Journal of Commonwealth Literature*, vol. 41, no.3, 2006, pp. 45–65.

Freud, Sigmund." Beyond the Pleasure Principle." *The Standard Edition of the Complete Psychological works of Sigmund Freud.* James Strachey. Hogarth Press.1953. pp.7-64

Freud, Sigmund. *The Psychopathology of Everyday Life.* General Press. 2018. Print

Kaul, Suvir. "Separation Anxiety: Growing Up Inter/National in Amitav Ghosh's "The Shadow Lines." *On India: Writing History, Culture, Post-Coloniality.* vol. 16. no. 1/2. 1994. pp. 125-145

Yusin, Jennifer. "The Silence of Partition: Borders, Trauma, and Partition history." *Social Semiotics,* vol. 19, no. 4, 2009, pp. 453-468

CHAPTER 11

Reframing the Roles: A Study of Shifting Narrative Strategies with Relation to Gender in Post Covid Malayalam Cinema

Akhila Ajith

Abstract

Cinema the most influencing of all entertainment media has often got claimed for its accustomed representations of stereotyped gender roles, religious ideologies, communities, cultural practices and more. This always made an enormous impact globally that unknowingly created and affected the lives of people. Notable among them is the aftermath caused on the gender roles directly dodge significant groups of people to the margin. Evidently, the gap it made between the gender especially men and women isolated the woman community as a whole into corners. The concept of gender became too stereotypical and attributed certain roles to it. Herein lies the transitional turn that got placed at the apt scenario. Within the last two decades, Malayalam cinema has been too experimental in its treatment of subjects, with courageous breaking down of the gender stereotypes and resultant gender roles. Never being too late to the changes, so many thoughtful reframing ideologies having hegemonic nature got completely destructed. To an extent the pandemic partly paralysed the film industry. But then a strong coming back actually paved a way to reach out to even more number of audience. The accessibility to a good number of films within the limits of home urged people to follow the medium than ever before. Film makers became too conscious and intelligent in creating a handful of wonderful contributions to the industry. The decade actually witnessed new transitions in the industry where a lot of novel themes and stories getting discussed. Even though the thematic framework may not change, the narrative strategies and portraying methods have undergone exceptional differences with relation to gender based reframing of roles. So this paper focuses on the reconstruction metamorphosis of gender roles with shifting narrative methods during post covid scenario.

Keywords: gender, stereotyped gender roles, reframing ideologies, shifting narrative strategies, post covid scenario, mollywood.

Introduction

Despite being a visual art and a powerful medium of communication that holds across the globe, movies stimulates and grasps a strong ascendancy on predisposing people and thereby the society itself into domain of novel perspectives. Accurately defined, "cinema is a matter of what's in the frame and what's out." Analysing apart from being too general while weighing up about the realm of films, the perception that Malayalam films have evolved into a refined and estimable level of change and aesthetic foundation has to be discussed in a wider perspective. The explicit reflection of what happens in the Malayalam film industry has been characterised by a handful of great and unusual themes, stories and narrative techniques. Even though the current transitional style furnishes several new trends and ideological outlooks that greatly differ from that of the thematic conventions of the past one or two decades, the aspect which makes it worth examining is that, while the new generation formats are largely dominated by the changing general and worldwide vogue, their total thematic structuring are deeply rooted within the Kerala or more specifically mallu lifestyle and mindscapes. One among the positive trendsetters that entered into Mollywood is its efforts to raise voice against the issues of gender equality, thereby shaping a novel sensibility and subtlety in normalising the gender justice. Glorifying patriarchal morality had been in practice of the industry as a trend that penetrated to and even from the cultural roots itself. Unapologetically Malayalam cinema celebrated it in various ways of character portrayals even very recently. When many of the film makers show reluctance to touch any of the grounds of sensitive subjects like these till date, comes some strong striking blow against prevailed misogyny and regressive ideologies through the transforming part of new wave Malayalam cinema. It is creating a context centered on dignity of individuals rather than the age old tradition of gender biased predispositions.

Article

Similar is the 2021 Sanu Varghese movie *Aarkariyam*, a story set against the backdrop of Covid lockdown. Apart from moving through a different subject treatment, the movie is a strong breaking of kitchen stereotypes that most of the family dramas reinforced.

The film is all about the life of a Mumbai based couple who get together with the wife's father when nationwide lockdown was proclaimed. Moving from a slow pace family story that gradually shapes into a thriller, the makers tried to reassure that their characters remained free from gender stereotypes. House making and taking care of the family that has always asserted as the only field of women has been gently overthrown throughout the film. Movie presents the three main characters sharing household chores, from cooking to all other duties without any hesitation. How the character Roy (husband), played by Sharafuddin looks after his father-in-law including his willingness to bathe the father and the way he treats the entire family matters seems to be new. Roy, also a step-father, got a unique presentation that stands against the cliched cruel and extremely negative step-father tradition. Equally or even more notable is the father role Ittiyavira played by Biju Menon, the so-called patriarchal head of the family who holds centrality of the story. He has been depicted as a very flexible and understanding man that again tries to bring forward an unusual thematic variance. The father figure always too stubborn and mostly occupying the personal choices of children especially daughters has literally got reconstructed even through the way he looks upon the second marriage of his daughter. By making the extraordinary as ordinary as possible, creators have brought an effortless 'change' into the limelight without amplifying or putting any extra conscious act to normalise things.

To the contrary, the critically acclaimed move *The Great Indian Kitchen* by Jeo Baby revolves around a typical household of Kerala where women, counting generations after the other, moil day and night. Highly reflecting the patriarchal indictment of marital life in India, the movie proposes how naturally women are constricted from achieving her own passions and desires. The opening scene of Nimisha Sajayan dancing and sweating stands as a symbol where she later sweats toiling in the kitchen throughout the film. The film has only two main male characters; the husband and the father-in-law, as classic representations of toxic masculinity. The husband, a school teacher who is simple and 'gentle' man displays the journey deep into the profundity of toxic marital life, tormenting his wife and act prejudiced in the bedroom. After all, in spite of having a respectable position of teacher who lives a life of independent nature from all aspects, he wants the life of women to be something entirely dedicated to make his tummy full with tasty food, sarcastically as what the title itself suggest. Not so different is the father-in-law figure who expects the daughter-in-law, after his wife to be the submissive housewife. Climax where the highly sensitive Sabarimala issue got mentioned, serves to a slap against male dominated marital institution of India. This film too again without glorifying reacts to patriarchal hold in families that has to undergo a change from the static rank of supremacy.

Again a highly discussed movie *Kala* by Rohith V.S. is a manifestation of hyper masculinity. Evidently, Shaji (Tovino Thomas), one of the main characters takes pride of his own virility that he consciously or unconsciously develops into danger. He with a strong pride celebrates the privileges he has amalgamating it with hyper masculinity. It starts from the very first scene itself where Shaji teaches his son to be a man who is not supposed to cry. Exaggerated masculinity where violence is treated as the vital manly indicative stands till the end. The perils of animal like cruelty are a less discussed topic and here it is almost like smelling flesh and blood. Again the picture of men with terrific energy and physical strength, exposed to violence that gives him the quality of being a man is something that is conveyed through the character Shaji. Shaji himself feels defeated only in the climax where he could realise his failure through his own perspective of a 'man'. The film is not just a remarkable comment on masculinity but have much more than that, which even reframes the concept of a protagonist always insisted with certain standards.

Above mentioned are a few that has to be seriously studied with regard to the explained discourse of Malayalam film industry. Not just one or two films stands responsible for the highly astounding transfigurations. Especially the past two years, the pandemic course of events contributed much more sophisticated films to the industry. While trying to interpret each and every movie serves to display multifaceted viewpoints which works exceptional based on their social relevance. Socially and culturally constructed norms influenced the audience to a great extent where politically correct ideas started getting sarcastically reviewed widely. Post pandemic era put forth a mesmerising metamorphosis to the existed false allegations and mindset of people. Without any clear reasons, the time witnessed sort of intellectual movement. May be the easiness that happened in the accessibility of more number of movies to more number of people gained its space of worth debating and study among themselves.

Accepting the view that all it started a decade ago, perhaps things got their right time and suitable spaces. Movies like *Kanekane, Home* etc. tries to bring the already detailed normalising 'changes'. The concept of how man and a woman should be got its new outlooks which make it too extraordinarily ordinary. The context of second marriages, where a step-mother and step-father having asserted with a bunch of characteristics and also the manner in which the family treat the couple varies from the conventionality has also been a remarkably significant. Notably an example, the movie *Kanekane* portrays a similar family. Even though belonging to a different genre, it tries to bring forth a few more progressive aspects that might valuably contribute to the society. It is getting thoroughly proved that mollywood is capable to restructure and reorganise the old space for misogyny, gender discrimination and injustice towards any gender without further considerations. Really going to witness a new aesthetic base with revolutionary ideals would make the process even more sensational.

Conclusion

The movies mentioned in the article are a few among a lot of the latest bunch presenting, desirable out of the box elements. In short standing still at a stage of repudiating the necessity of questioning affairs related to gender and equality, we witness clear transformations happening that impacts the emergence of new discourses getting established through several characters and movies. All these mark the strength of exceptional delineations of themes focusing gender equality, justice, individuality and conveying them in a manner which is too subtle and precise to analyse or describe.

Works cited

Mathew, Soumya. *Ananlysing Body, Anatomy &Gendered spaces in The Great Indian Kitchen,* February 1 2021, www.google.com&ampshare=http%3A%2A%2Afeminisnindia.com. Accessed 16 June 2022.

V. P, Karishma. *Film review: The Great Indian Kitchen – serbing patriarchy, Piping* Hot!, January 18 2021,https://feminisminindia.com. Accessed 16 June 2022.

CHAPTER 12

Food as a Tool for Identity: A Study of Food and Diaspora in Bharti Kirchner's *Pastries*

Apoorva Poonia

Abstract

Beyond simple nourishment, facts that "what we eat", "how we eat", "with whom we eat" and even "when we eat"' seeps in the manner we are judged in a given social setting. It becomes even more pronounced in cases of migrants and diasporic settings. Inadvertently, food shows up in their everyday lives as a mighty background of their 'productive' activities and hence literature profusely uses these gastro – symbols to be able to paint higher meanings of nostalgia, acculturation and identity formation. Kirchner's narratives have made very imaginative use of this gastro-symbolism to enrich her literary oeuvre. Her works like *Shiva Dancing*, *Sharmila's Book*, *Darjeeling* etc. are abound with food images and symbols. This research paper is called "Food as a Tool for Identity: A Study of Food and Diaspora in Bharti Kirchner's *Pastries*" and it focuses on how the culinary images, symbols and dietary choices of a person shape up the sense of self and build one's identity in Bharti Kirchner's novel *Pastries*. It shall use the tool of diaspora to analyse the intertwined complexities of narrative structure, thematic build-up and meaning creation in the novel. This exploratory approach shall conjoin food, diaspora and identity building to reach to its conclusion that in *Pastries*, Kirchner uses food in ways more than just that of survival for the characters Sunya Malhotra and her mother, Mrs. Deepika Malhotra.

Keywords: Food, Bharti Kirchner, Pastries, Diaspora, Identity, Memory, Nostalgia

Introduction

People use food in ways more than just sustenance. It shapes their understanding of others on grounds of culture and race, ethico-political environment and region and nationality; thereby outlining one's identity. Psychoanalytical theorists such as Jennifer Burcham

Whitt also suggests in her research article titled "An Appetite for Metaphor: Food Imagery and Cultural Identity in Indian Fiction" (2011) that our eating methods are significant to our construction of self-identity and also in others' perception of ourselves (Appetite). One of the very famous food metaphors concerning identity is the Bible's usage of bread in reference to Jesus Christ. It says, "And Jesus said unto them, I am the bread of life; he that cometh to me shall never hunger; and he that believeth on me shall never thirst" (John 6:35). Jesus compares himself to bread and absorbs the symbol of sustenance, using food as a metaphor for his own body. Mohandas Karamchand Gandhi's vegetarianism, the greased cartridges (of beef and pig fat) rebellion of the 1857, 'famine-fictions' of Mahashweta Devi have proven the deep and fascinating connection food has with the larger social and global issues. This paper focuses on how food helps shape up identities of the leading characters of novel *Pastries: A Novel of Desserts and Discoveries* by Bharti Kirchner.

Chapter

Bharti Kirchner is an Indian born and Seattle based diasporic novelist and cookbook writer. Born in 1940, she migrated to the States in her young years and has penned numerous articles, essays and novels on issues galore. Her writings fiercely depict her displaced heroines' efforts to integrate their lost cultural identity directly or indirectly emerging out of an aroused direct contact with the past. She also significantly portrays how these characters feel one with their 'own' food. It is most pungently captured in *Pastries* (2003) where the protagonist Sunya Malhotra is a second generation migrant who is based in the city of Seattle of United States of America. Sunya has a typical Indian mother, Deepika Malhotra who incessantly keeps the connection with food alive throughout the narrative. Sub – titled as '*A Novel of Desserts and Discoveries*', *Pastries* is mainly a story of Sunya Malhotra who has transformed her love for bakery into an art through her cakes and pastries. She lives with her Indian mother Deepika who is the foundation of Sunya's personality today. The foodways presented in the narrative are poignant in forming identities of both the women. Foodways refers to the ways of eating one's food. It is the analysis of how, what, with whom, when and why a person consumes food. So, foodways becomes an inclusive term for one's culture, commensality and customs related to food.

The vortex of the story of *Pastries* is baking. For both Sunya and her mother, cooking activities like baking, making donuts, cakes, pies etc. are their source of livelihood, passion and a medium of identity formation. Sunya, for example, is a renowned baker and the owner of Pastries Café while Mrs. Malhotra's donuts shop has its own fanbase. But food images other than baking also are very relevant for a deeper understanding of food and identity in the select narrative.

Food operates on two levels with Deepika Malhotra. Firstly, her American identity as a small-scale but famous donut shop owner. Secondly, keeping her Indian identity alive through use of certain gastro memory-triggers like spices, mangoes etc. This paper shall discuss them one by one. She owns a small donut shop in her Seattle neighborhood that has no dearth of loyal customers. Deepika's donut shop is applauded by Sunya's love interest Andrew in the following lines where he says:

> Fortunately, after much walking around I stumbled upon a donut shop with the most beautiful silk curtains on the windows … served the most wonderful cinnamon donuts. I've never tasted anything like this, not even in New York. Every morning I used to run up there and order a couple of donuts at a time. (67)

Andrew remembers how the white frosting of Deepika's donuts stuck to his fingers and how I licked it all off. He cannot forget the delicious taste her donuts had to offer and calls it "the greatest discovery on that trip" (67). For Deepika, her donuts gifted people sweet mornings and so Bharti Kirchner stretches the meaning of donuts to sweet gifts as good luck tokens. Kirchner narrates that Deepika, like Santa Claus with her fresh and warm donuts "brought cheer to the textureless mornings of so many souls" (69). Her donut shop is so fiercely intertwined with Deepika's construction of self that many times in her working life, she fought and fought to keep her donut shop against bigger outfits. The donut shop is the symbolic station of dreams, identity and future of both the women. Even Sunya feels that her "mother's donut shop was an incubator for dreams I cherished, those I hold even today" (54). Even if Deepika retired from her donut shop, she reminds Sunya about her connection with baking while cheering her up about the bakery war saying "That was my dream, too, to have a full bakery" (53).

Food also associates Deepika with her Indian past. Throughout the novel we see the 'Indian' in Sunya's mother through nostalgic flashbacks and Indian food. Indian movies, Indian festivals, culture and Indian food hold an added importance for migrants like Deepika Malhotra for it is a reason to hold on to the roots and their importance can never be over-emphasised. Sunya's mother is a typical Indian born-and-brought-up woman who still clings on to the values fervently. Sunya has seen her mother worship Indian movies – "fillim as they pronounce" and these Indian films become an escape from the mundane life of every Indian woman living in the West and even the Indian diasporic society at large (45). Her kitchen is loaded with rich spices from India like saffron because she knew the cultural importance and health benefits of the spices. Elios Joseph and Robert Voeks in their 2021 article "Indian Diaspora Gastronomy: On the Changing Use of Herbs and Spices Among Southern California's Indian Immigrant Women" also say that food distinguishes Indians from the rest in a very pronounced manner. They write, "their use of herbs and spices in food and medicine, in particular, is tightly bound to language, religion, gender, and overall cultural identity" (Gastronomy). Even in other narratives of Kirchner, the presence of Indian spices in the kitchen of the migrants is vividly present. Her characters enjoy cooking and so does Mrs. Malhotra. Even while cooking she always hummed some Indian song. Even the curtains of her small donut shop had curtains that were made out of her silk saris.

Therefore, food forms the identity of Deepika on two levels. First, financially as she had to start a small business to support her family after her husband abandoned her. Secondly, personally or culturally as Bengali food keeps her connection with her native roots alive. In one of the episodes, Deepika makes a lavish Indian (Bengali) dinner for her guests Dushan and Cartdale. She chooses to make "*mangsho*" and Cartdale can't help relishing it. He liked the *mangsho* so much that he ended up taking three servings. Deepika is also famous for the lamb curry she makes. Similarly, a sweet dish called *kachagolla* has been repeatedly used as Deepika's culinary masterpiece in India. Deepika's mother associates her identity with this food, calling it "Dee's ethereal version" (148).

There are many narratives whose protagonists feel the dilemma of acculturation and tossing between the western food and Indian food. Though Deepika does not feel any frustration adjusting to the American ways, some people do feel the transition very challenging. In Kiran Desai's *Inheritance of Loss* (2006) for example, the protagonist Biju succumbs to this transition process, called acculturation which is necessary for a sound settlement into the new host land, and returns to India. The critical works and theoretical framework of Anita Mannur in her *Culinary Fictions: Food in South Asian Diasporic Culture* (2009), Vijay Mishra in *The Diasporic Imaginary and the Indian Diaspora* (2005) and Parama Roy in *Alimentary Tracts: Appetites, Aversions, and the Postcolonial* (2010) highlight the role of foodways in the cultural manifestation of the Indian diaspora. They prove that food embodies more than just one set of meaning. Writers like Salman Rushdie, Anita Desai, Timothy Mo, V. S. Naipaul, Kiran Desai, etc. have depicted various cultural, racial and national ambiguities, incongruities and contradictions, many of which have been narrated using food imagery.

How Sunya's individuality in *Pastries* is represented in the eyes of people is clear from the fact that filmmaker Andrew declares to Sunya that "I can see that you've obviously inherited your mother's talents" and that opening up Pastries Café was a good career choice (67). Even as a young girl, Sunya's love for cooking is seen in the fact that she would help her mother with her donut shop. This childhood training brought about a phenomenal change in Sunya with the fact that she took to baking as a spiritual task – the proof of it being her phenomenal Sunya Cake.

Sunya cake is a symbolic representation of Sunya's identity as a baker. This cake is the manifestation of her professional excellence and therefore it forms an undeniably inseparable component of Sunya's personality. Filmmaker Andrew in a lighthearted manner says that Sunya cake is Sunya 'herself' and vice-versa. He further equates her special cake with Sunya herself saying, "if this were a movie, practitioners of that order would be after your Sunya Cake recipe because it's their namesake. In effect, they'd be after you" (95). Sunya's possessiveness about the cake shows that it is more than just a dish. She says, "because Sunya cake is so famous, and so I've kept its recipe secret. Every business has its treasured possessions" and calls the recipe her "company jewels" (85). Sunya believes that Sunya cake is her whole identity and her reason for survival in this otherwise competitive capitalist bakery world.

The recipe of Sunya's cake is worth stealing in the narrative. This food-item has been given a very unique treatment because of the experience it gives after its consumption. Sunya's friend Roger, pronounces Sunya's signature creation as something having a "transcendental experience" (120). Sunya's café is very famous in the locality and has a good number of customers. Banking on the market created by Sunya single handedly, the famous chain of Cakes Plus wants to open up their chain of café, giving her a very daunting competition. During this bakery war we see Sunya's stress build up so much that it affects her identity and she loses confidence many times. This exerts an influence on her baking skills and she stops baking her signature Sunya Cake. To revive her baker's identity, she signs up for a course in Kyoto, Japan. This section of the narrative comprehensively proves how food is more than just an edible substance. For Sunya, the baking classes at Kyoto under the auspices of the baker guru Matsumoto are transforming. She decides that on her return, she'll be ready to give Sunya cake a new life. She has the whole project planned in her mind. During her course at Kyoto, she further learns that the identity defining virtues of non-attachment, contentment and being "one with baking" apply to cooking/baking also.

Food is a pronounced mark of uncovering the Malhotras' ethnicity as well as identity and authors like Bharti Kirchner specify food as a primary way of identifying characters with their aboriginal homes and cultures. This food is both Indian and also somewhat American, for both mother and daughter are bakers. Deepika Malhotra uses Indian food to make herself feel "homely" in a gastronomically "unhomely" territory. She further uses it to maintain her daughter's touch with Indian food culture. These ways of preserving one's personal (and yet collective) culture has been termed as "chutnification of history" by Salman Rushdie, when he narrates similar attempts to maintain and preserve native culture in his famous *Midnight's Children* (1981). In the novel, the big pickled mango jars represent the characters' preserved and valuable Indian culture. Loosely called "pickl-ify", these gastro-acts are native to Indian foodways and involve a cooking process that is able to preserve food for a very long time – like pickles, chutneys (preserved dips in English), *murabbas* (marmalades) etc. Like certain spices and oil is added to food to preserve it, a migrant inculcates certain habits that preserves his culture – like his religion, food choices and habits (like eating with bare hands), language etc. Rushdie says:

> One day, perhaps, the world may taste the pickles of history. They may be too strong for some palates, their smell may be overpowering, tears may rise to eyes; I hope nevertheless that it will be possible to say of them that they possess the authentic taste of truth … that they are, despite everything, acts of love. (qtd in Crane 170)

In *Pastries*, romantic intricacies also revolve around food, important discussions happen over food, filmmaker Andrew weaves and then shares his story over food and almost every single flashback reminiscence besides food making the title perfectly apt for the story. Then food also becomes a way of judging other's identity. For example, in one of the episodes, there is a mention to the symbol of the fruit pomegranate. In Andrew's house is kept a half-eaten pomegranate fruit sitting in the shadow of a tall canister on the counter. The fruit holds a special meaning in Andrew's life and Sunya's perception about Andrew after this incident. Inspired by the Dutch painter's painting of a pomegranate, Andrew bought this showpiece from California. For him, "a pomegranate stood for hope" (277). The oldest religious texts of Hinduism, the Vedas, also consider this fruit a powerful symbol of fertility and good health.

People also form a judgment about other people on the basis of their food habits. During a dinner table discussion, Sunya mentions some Dr. Hussain "who couldn't tell the difference between naan and kulcha" (69). This ignorance about the basics of his own native food has given him the title of "food-illiterate" by the Indian community.

Another powerful (and perhaps Kirchner's favorite) is tea symbolism. In other narratives of Kirchner too, like *Darjeeling* (2002), *Sharmila's Book* (1999) and *Shiva Dancing* (1998) we find a lot of tea motifs and related culinary symbols. Tea becomes a powerful source of narration driving and a motif of characters' nostalgia in *Pastries*. She meets Andrew for the first time and he orders for an iced '*chai*' – the Indian name for tea. Sunya remembers and hence narrates the entire section of flashback while sipping the Indian tea. Infact, an entire chapter is dedicated to Sunya sipping her tea and casting her mind to the father's abandoning them. Andrew has been shown making important decisions sipping *chai* in her café. Later in another chapter, Sunya is sitting with her mother and sipping her *chai* when the mother recalls Prabhu's routine; how he started from his house sharp at eight in the morning with a bulging briefcase in hand, walked across the street to the store at the entrance to the alley. It is in the same chapter when the mother is shown zapping through the old album of her paternal grandmother along with sipping tea. Again, they remember their Indian days and its culture, "the faith they had in their adopted land" (213).

About *chai*, the most remarkably exciting scene cannot be missed. It is in the ending chapters, when Bikkhu Karun waves toward the tea set and Sunya lifts the cup to her lips with both hands and takes another sip. The two are shown sipping tea when their identity is disclosed. Symbolically, tea holds a very integral part in the lives of the characters. Sunya shares with the readers the important role food plays in the lives of Indian people and culture and how it shaped their identities. Even love between Andrew and Sunya develops over food which Kirchner calls "the symbiotic bond between the pastry practitioner and the consumer." (64). To Sunya, food was life. She says, "to me food is order, sanity, as Pierre would call it, intimate…to steal a glance at the next table's order. To taste and judge what my peers are concocting. To be inspired. To kick back and just be. (89)

Conclusion

The essence of food metaphor in literature and culture therefore is based on the connection of consumption with identity. This kind of comparison occurs for the reason that each culture has within itself a systematic organisation of food. Mary Duglas in *Deciphering a Meal* (1975) says that food always carries a symbolic value and has a meaning. She says, "The meaning of a meal is found in a system of repeated analogies. Each meal carries something of the meaning of the other meals; each meal is a structured social event which structures others in its own image" (260). Postmodern society believes in choosing their own identity rather than following the one ascribed to them and therefore, the literature becomes colored in newer imagery, metaphors and symbols to give way to deeper meanings. This approach is based on the fact that human relationship with food is very complex.

Food can have different meanings for different people. Their identities can be connected to food in a varied manner. In a cinematic representation called *Mirchi Malini* (2018), Pratim D. Gupta takes "we are what we eat" literally by portraying a woman who is a food astrologer. She predicts one's future by tasting the food cooked by him/her. Similarly, Bharti Kirchner's *Pastries* use culinary motifs and symbols that personifies food (both consumption and preparation) and lends a particular identity to its protagonists. This intertwining of food and identity makes *Pastries* a love story with the fact that Sunya would do anything to save the love of her life, that is baking and Mrs. Malhotra would never let the love for cooking die. Food makes their social recognition stronger because apart from cooking at home to feed their loved ones, Sunya and Deepika also associate with food as their wholesome financial support and bread and butter, literally. The novel also proves the characters' attempts to "pickle time" in order to address their diasporic memory thereby defining their Indian identities. "Food as a Tool for Identity: A Study of Food and Diaspora in Bharti Kirchner's *Pastries*" thus attempts to prove that food operates on multi-level in this story – on financial, emotional, diasporic, spiritual and naturally on corporeal levels. Culinary symbols invariably remain in the backdrop of the novel shaping the identities of the protagonists.

Works Cited

Crane, Ralph J. "The Chutnification of History." *Inventing India, SpringerLink*, 1992, link.springer.com/chapter/10.1057/9780230380080_8.

Das, Angshuman. "Mango and Masala: Food in the Immigrant Novel." *The Ploughshares Blog,* blog.pshares.org/index.php/mango-and-masala-food-in-the-immigrant-novel/.

Douglas, Mary. "Deciphering a Meal." *Food and Culture*, vol. 101, no. 1, 1972, pp. https://www.jstor.org/stable/20024058. Accessed 18 May 2022.

Joseph, Elois, and Robert Voeks. "Indian Diaspora Gastronomy: On the Changing Use of Herbs and Spices Among Southern California's Indian Immigrant Women." *Frontiers in Sustainable Food Systems*, doi: https://doi.org/10.3389/fsufs.2021.610081.

John 6:35. biblehub.com/john/6-35.html.

Kirchner, Bharti. *Pastries: A Novel of Desserts and Discoveries.* St. Martin's Griffin, 2004.

Whitt, Jennifer Burcham. "An Appetite For Metaphor: Food Imagery And Cultural Identity In Indian Fiction." *(Department of English) East Carolina University*, May 2011,
thescholarship.ecu.edu/bitstream/handle/10342/3535/Whitt_ecu_0600M_10386.pdf?sequence=1&isAllowed=y.

CHAPTER 13

The Contagion of "Fallenness": The Portrayal of Prostitution in Charles Dickens' *Oliver Twist* and Leo Tolstoy's *Resurrection*

Jagari Mukherjee

Abstract

Prostitution is often referred to as the social evil but the Victorians took their condemnation of it to new heights. Many of the women involved were there through no fault of their own, but once "fallen," they would not have been welcomed back to their homes – regardless of the cause of their fall. True, some chose the profession, but some were kidnapped, and some worked due to poverty. The sympathetic author Charles Dickens co-founded Urania Cottage, a shelter for fallen women, and wove the stories of these women into his novels. On the other hand, Leo Tolstoy wrote *Resurrection* to raise enough money for a persecuted community known as the *Doukhobors*, to enable the members of the community to emigrate to Canada. Both *Oliver Twist* and *Resurrection* are memorable for their depiction of fallen women and their ill-treatment at the hands of society. The hypocritical attitude of European society towards these fallen women is a thread that connects these texts. The belief that fallen women are a contaminating agent pervaded nineteenth-century European society and deserves to be examined.

Keywords: Contagion, Fallen Women, Prostitute, Nancy, Katyusha, Nineteenth-century novel

Introduction

The Chapter proposes to "fallen women" as agents of social contagion in two nineteenth-century novels, with reference to the female protagonists of these novels. These are Nancy from *Oliver Twist (1839)* by Charles Dickens and Katyusha Maslova from *Resurrection (1899)* by Leo Tolstoy.

The two texts selected for this chapter is based on a couple of factors. Firstly, these texts gained both popularity and notoriety on their publication for the sympathetic treatment by the (male) authors of fallen women. These novels are popular even to this day, thereby serving as an evidence of the attraction harboured towards the topic of fallen women by readers and writers alike. Secondly, although these two novels were published in different countries, different languages, and across a few decades, both serve to highlight society's hypocritical attitude towards fallen women through a variety of characters' reactions in the novels.

The term "fallen woman", according to Amanda Anderson, is a "wide umbrella term for varying female identities, meaning that we should acknowledge the fluidity of being fallen because the variety of identities allocated to the fallen identity itself connotes a lack of fixture to pre-existing cultural codes." On the other hand, Lynda Nead makes a distinction between a "fallen woman" and a "prostitute" in so far as the terms are dependent on class – the former belongs to upper or middle class, and her sexual indiscretion, leading to her fall, has no link to her financial requirement, whereas the latter belongs to a lower-class and are monetarily independent, often seen as victims of circumstances and therefore objects of compassion. However, for the purpose of this paper, the term "fallen woman" will be used as a broad umbrella term.

In the nineteenth century, fallen women were often viewed as agents of social contamination. Richard Broad, of Royal Holloway, University of London, in his thesis *Water and the Fallen Woman in Victorian Literature and Art,* explores the relationship between the fallen woman and water as a polluting agent in *David Copperfield*, *Ruth*, and G. F. Watt's painting *Found Drowned.* In Michele Roberts' article published in *The Guardian* titled "The fallen woman: prostitution in literature", she takes the example of Emile Zola's courtesan heroine, Nana, who rises from her working-class origins as a virus and infects upper-class society in her lust for sex.

Let us now examine the two characters under discussion for this paper.

Nancy

Nancy is introduced to us, along with her friend Bet, as a member of Fagin's gang of criminals in Chapter 9 of *Oliver Twist.* Her untidy appearance, the heavily rouged and made-up face, dirty shoes and socks leave no doubt in the mind of the reader as her identity as a prostitute. Oliver, an innocent ten-year old, thinks of them as "very nice girls indeed." This is followed by the author's ironical remark, "As there is no doubt they were." (69). Nancy's appearance gives an impression of dirt, filth and disease, a moral contagion in society. Charley Bates and the Artful Dodger, who are young boys themselves, go off with Nancy and Bet, having been corrupted as children. This is a portent of Oliver's future – thieving and dallying with prostitutes – if he stayed on with the group.

Nancy has been thieving for Fagin ever since she is five years old, and living with Bill Sikes for many years. She had fallen since her childhood, and her innocence destroyed from early on. Thus, she helps the gang by kidnapping Oliver from the bookstall, dressing up as a respectable woman searching for her missing brother. Yet, as the novel progresses, Nancy begins to change in the face of Oliver's goodness and innocence. Dickens shows his readers that even a fallen woman has a tender heart.

Other than a tender heart, Nancy also has a conscience. She is acutely and painfully conscious of the shame and sin which define her life, and color even her good qualities. She saves Oliver from being beaten by Fagin after he is brought back (120). At that moment, her conscience is aroused and "her passion was frightful to see." She screams at Fagin, "I thieved for you when I was a child not half as old as this!..." When Fagin attempts to pacify her by saying that she now has a living, Nancy retorts, "It is my living; and the cold, wet, dirty streets are my home…". The cold, wet and dirty streets of London during Victorian England are conducive to the spread of both physical and moral contagion. The world around Nancy is an insalubrious one. She, in spite of the goodness of her heart, is trapped in a diseased milieu and there is no escape for her.

We see how harshly Nancy is judged by so-called respectable folks when she goes to meet Rose Maylie at a hotel for the first time. While the man servant hesitates to carry her message to Miss Maylie, four "chaste" housemaids affirm that Nancy is a disgrace to her sex and should be thrown into the dog kennel. They are not way off the mark as Nancy's relationship with Bill Sikes is abusive and he treats her worse than he treats his dog. Yet, Nancy is infatuated with Sikes and refuses the help offered by Rose; and as a consequence, goes to her doom. Later on in the book, the kind Mr Brownlow offers asylum to Nancy. Yet, Nancy has gone far beyond the realm of hope and has fallen into despair. When Rose, full of pity, cries out that what could be the end of Nancy's life, the latter shows her the dark waters of the Thames river, says that those like her usually "spring into the tide." Nancy has a grim foreboding of her death. While waiting to go out to meet Rose and Mr Brownlow, she is haunted by disturbing mental images and sees the word "Coffin" written across her book. Sadly, when Death comes for her, it is not of her choosing.

As this researcher has reiterated before, a fallen woman is said to infect society, and thus is removed from society by her death. Nancy's case is a terrifying reminder that not all prostitutes end up being saved, and that all fallen women are not as fortunate as Emily and Martha from Dickens' own *David Copperfield*. When Death finally arrives for Nancy, she meets it at the hands of the man she loves, who violently clubs her and murders her. The pus-filled, infected wound of society explodes, blinded by its own blood.

Katyusha

The French Noble Prize winner, Romain Rolland, described Tolstoy's novel *Resurrection* as "one of the most beautiful poems of human compassion; perhaps the most truthful ever written." Katyusha Maslova, an innocent girl, is seduced by Dmitri Nekhyudov at the age of sixteen, gives birth to a child who does not survive, and lives with one 'protector' after the other before turning to prostitution. Her moral degeneration begins along with her loss of physical purity; she is forced by circumstances to become a prostitute, but she also hands over her passport to the procuress because the latter tempts her that she can order any kinds of dresses that she wants. Katyusha succumbs to the temptation like Eve succumbs to Satan, visualising herself in a yellow silk dress with black trimmings (13).

Tolstoy does not gloss over the sordid details of a prostitute's life. He describes the daily rituals of Maslova's degraded existence in intricate detail, from her getting up wearily from a dirty bed at three or four o' clock, to the night-time debauchery with all sorts of men thus painting a picture of unwholesomeness. The writer also warns that such a life ends for nine out of ten women in painful disease, premature decrepitude and death. This moral degeneration has spread like contagion across all ranks of society. It is the culmination of the spread of this moral contagion that results in Katyusha being accused of poisoning one of her clients. At her trial, Nekhlyudov, her seducer, is on the jury and recognises her. His conscience is aroused, and he is resurrected as a good human being. However, Maslova, although she is innocent, is found guilty and exiled to four years' penal servitude in Siberia. At first, she is not moved by Nekhlyudov's repentance. She tells him, "You've used me for your pleasure in this life, and you want to use me to get salvation in the world to come."(190) The contagion has seeped so deeply in her soul that it is difficult for her to change her ways soon. It is only slowly that she begins to love and trust Nekhlyudov again, and brings about positive changes in herself.

Nekhlyudov becomes a Christ-like figure to Katyusha's Mary Magdalene, and attempts to save her from being exiled to Siberia. However, the novel is replete with images of sickness, disease and death. The scenes set in the prison to which Maslova is sent are harrowing, with ill and miserable prisoners treated badly by the authorities. Nekhlyudov determines to follow Maslova to Siberia and offers to marry her to redeem his own original sin.

It is through Nekhlydov that the healing from the moral contagion begins. Following Nekhlyudov's petition, Maslova is sent to the prison hospital to work as a nurse. Henceforth, she becomes an agent of optimistic change and recovery. Later on, Maslova helps out other weaker, more unfortunate women prisoners and takes care of them, sometimes appealing to Nekhlyudov to aid them in their times of distress. At the end, Maslova rejects Nekhlyudov's proposal of marriage and decides to accept the proposal of a political prisoner named Simonson who is in love with her. The once-fallen Katyusha Maslova rises in our esteem with her act of self-sacrifice. She loves Nekhlyudov, but does not want to marry him because she knows that he, being a prince, would lose his place of respect in society if he marries a former prostitute. She does not want to contaminate Nekhlyudov's position by associating herself closely with him. The novel ends with Nekhlydov alone in his room reading from the Bible, saved and purified.

Conclusion

The basis of the concept of fallen women is the norms of sexual purity imposed upon them in the nineteenth century, both in Victorian England and elsewhere in Europe. The subject has been a source of fascination for major novelists. The unjust treatment meted out to fallen women is prevalent even to this day. In its extreme form, one has witnessed the barbaric custom of "honor killing", where women like Qandeel Baloch are murdered by their own family members because of their perceived fallen state. By revisiting these two texts the paper will bring into discourse the recurring nature of the subjugation of woman through the creation of stereotypes. Thereby, the paper will add to the pedagogy of gender studies by relooking at the archive and making it relevant so that the amnesia induced by a patriarchal structure in order to sustain its dominance is negated. My paper will also invite further research in the domain of literature to reiterate the need for an epistemological shift from male-centric literary discourse.

Even today, the concept of fallen women exists in many societies. Sexual purity is still insisted upon as the norm for women, not for men, and women deviating from this norm, even when it is not by their choice, are treated in a harsh and unjust manner. The two novels, *Oliver Twist* and *Resurrection,* may end differently for the two fallen women, but the common thread of lost innocence and social disgrace connect both of them. Today, just as in the nineteenth-century, there is a greater need to change the patriarchal narrative of fallen women. While Dickens' Nancy serves as a terrible warning to fallen women in 1839, Tolstoy's Katyusha is the harbinger of hope and healing sixty years later, in 1899. The contagion has abated, and in the twenty-first century, we can hope, and take steps, to move only forward.

Works Cited

Anderson, Amanda. *Tainted Souls and Painted Faces: The Rhetoric of Fallenness in Victorian Culture*, Cornell University Press, 1993.

Bayley, John. *Tolstoy And The Novel.* Chatto & Windus. 1966.

Broad, Richard. *Water and the Fallen Woman in Victorian Literature and Art.* 2011, Royal Holloway, University of London, MA thesis. www.academia.edu/1505231.

Dickens, Charles. *David Copperfield.* Bantam Dell, 2006.

Dickens, Charles. *Oliver Twist.* Wordsworth Editions, 1992.

Nead, Lynda. *Myths of Sexuality: Representations of Women in Victorian Britain,* Basil Blackwell, 1988.

Roberts, Michele. "The fallen woman: prostitution in literature." *The Guardian,* 14 April 2017,www.theguardian.com/books/2017/apr/14/the-fallen-woman-prostitution-in-literature.

Rolland, Romain. *Life of Tolstoy.* Translated by Bernard Niall. Adelphi Terrace, 1911.

CHAPTER 14

Analysing Opportunities for Women in Journalism with Reference to Susannah Cahalan's novel *Brain on Fire: My Month of Madness*

Biju Chetia and Daisy Priya Gogoi

Abstract

Discrimination against women has been witnessed from time immemorial. Perhaps Virginia Woolf couldn't have been more right when she stressed on how the conditions that a woman is exposed to affects her identity. With the advancement of time, technology and science have seen huge progress. However, the stereotypical mindset of the patriarchal society still remains unchanged. In this paper, the discrimination faced by women in the world of journalism shall be analysed through an indepth reading of Susannah Cahalan's illness narrative *Brain on Fire: My Month of Madness*. The work describes the competition and the insecurities that haunted Cahalan, most of which were directly affected by the pressure in her field of work. Women are doubly pressured – firstly because of the competition in the workplace, and secondly because they are judged on the basis on their gender. Along with Cahalan's work, other texts of writers shall also be analysed where they speak on how the women face discrimination in the world of journalism, a profession dominated by males. Moreover, the media present an image of a perfect woman which comes at the expense of the true woman that possesses equal capabilities and talent as males. As a reporter herself, Cahalan expresses the challenges she faces in her line of work while suffering from NMDA-autoimmune encephalitis.

Keywords: women, journalism, discrimination, inequality, patriarchy.

Article

> "Women have served all these centuries as looking glasses possessing the magic and delicious power of reflecting the figure of man at twice its natural size." – Virginia Woolf.

Indeed the potential possessed by a woman is in no way inferior to men. They have the equal capabilities and capacity to achieve greatness as men. However, in the world of literature throughout history women are seen striving a lot to gain an equal focus like their male counterpart. The cause of the less exposure of women's capacities does not lie in the women themselves, but lies in the system prevalent in society – the patriarchal system. It is the system that had denied proper education for women in the past. Men have always got access to proper institutions where they could expand their knowledge and learn new ideas. They were praised as intellectuals for their writings and research. However, perhaps we would never know if women of the time were equally or perhaps even more talented than them since they were never provided with the similar facilities. They were confined to their homes, made to take responsibility of the domestic household and denied a proper institution to harness their skills. The work *A Room of One's Own* by Virginia Woolf is a seminal text which provides apt and clear picture of how the talent and intellectual genius in women get ignored and lost in the patriarchal society. She describes how it is unthinkable for any woman in Shakespeare's day to become a 'genius' because society would never let her get the chance to express herself. Even if she possessed remarkable qualities, she would never be provided with the platform or opportunity to hone her skills and master them. Furthermore, for instance, a woman who possessed knowledge of herbs and medicine would rather be looked at as a witch rather than a genius. They were not seen in the same light as men. Even though society has moved beyond that mentality in today's age, women continue to be treated as 'damsels' and are undermined.

Women faced great inequalities in the past. They were always regarded as beings that are sentimental, incapable of genius and rationality like men. In modern times such discrimination, although reduced, has not become extinct even in the 21st century. Discrimination of women exists in every facet of life. They are treated as a "second sex" as Simeon de Beauvoir writes in her book The Second Sex. Man defines a woman's identity instead of a woman being able to define her role in the society. They get labeled as someone's wife, someone's daughter or someone's mother. However, their own individuality and identity gets lost. She becomes a silenced voiced and is pushed to the background, despite her contribution to the family or the society at large. Beauvoir, in her book, writes how "humanity is male" and it is the man that "defines woman, not in herself". She is defined not with her own unique identity, "but in relation to himself". She is defined according to the domestic role she plays and by praising her nurturing and compassionate nature, the society in a way tries to condition women into thinking that they are being acknowledged. However, in reality, it is actually a shackle disguised as a compliment to prevent them from protesting to the gender biased norms. These are the qualities that are expected of a 'good woman'. Her own identity as an individual with intellect, skill and reasoning is ignored, just because she is a woman.

Men have always played the superior role and tried to dominate women. This exists not only limited to the literary sphere, but also extends to the sphere of journalism. Journalism, by nature, is not gendered. However, the reaction of society towards male and female journalist is what makes the bias and the discrimination obvious. As Dr. I. Shivakumar rightly states "Women Journalists fail to show up their own creation by facing internal and external gender discrimination." (58)

Professions like medicine and journalism are considered highly male and across various societies, the amount of males is more as compared to men. This detail is can be successfully backed up by the "Global Report on the Status of Women in the News Media" published by the IWMF (International Women's Media Foundation). The report notes that "men represent nearly two-thirds (64.9%) of the total workforce across regions, compared to slightly more than one-third women (35.1%)." The media is one of the sources which pose as a barrier, as well as a means through which women empowerment could either is limited or they could be encouraged. Provided the right message and the opportunity, females could be encourage to take up more bold professions like journalism and the field of medicine. However, it often happens that women are commodified and they are represented as objects, rather than individuals with their own opinions, thoughts and intellect. The change in the field of journalism would ensure an overall change in the stereotypes against women. "The most significant and longest social movement" mentions Ray in his work, is "movement for emancipation of women. Though the primary goal for women empowerment is to improve the quality of life of women but it has also deep ramifications in social, economic and political scenario of body polity."

Suzanne Franz in her article, *Women and Journalism*, notes how there is a stark contrast in the number of women who join institutions offering courses in journalism, as compared to the number of successful journalists who spring up. She writes how women join in more numbers but the outcome doesn't match the effort. High profession jobs in mass communication and promotions are often more noticed in case of male candidates rather than female. The pay scale also has differences when it comes to both genders. Suzanne Franz notes how the amount of women who pursue a career in journalism is actually higher than men. However, when it comes to job opportunities and pay scale, there is a huge difference. The male candidates get more pay and also better opportunities than females. Furthermore, the more breaks women take, the more difficult it becomes for them to regain the little progress they made in the field of journalism. This is seen in many Western countries as noted by Franz.

The media is, in a way, the constructor of the social expectations that forms in the minds of the people. The ideas that they preach, the products that they advertise influence the society, especially the youth. The media crafts an image of the idealwoman and objectifies them and presents them to the world as a commodity. The profession of journalism is in itself a male dominated profession where misogyny and stereotypes against women could almost be considered banal. In the article, "Women and News: Making Connections between the Global and the Local" by Geertsema, she discusses the problems faced by women in the world of media and journalism:

> ...while female journalists around the world made some inroads during the 1980s, their position in the media deteriorated since the mid-1990s. Yet, even when female reporters enter newsrooms, the content of news does not necessarily become more gender sensitive. On the other hand, male reporters are also able to report news from a gender perspective. (Geertsema 4)

The female reporters have to work twice as hard as the males for their promotion and acknowledgement. Moreover, the image that the media presents of women is distorted. They present the women in a way that would serve their own interests.

In her autobiographical work *Brain on Fire: My Month of Madness*, Susannah Cahalan writes about her experience as a journalist while suffering from a rare neurological disease namely, N-methyl-D-asparatate receptor encephalitis, also referred to as NMDA autoimmune encephalitis. It is a disease that creates antibodies against the NMDA – receptors in the brain due to which swelling of the brain or other such brain dysfunctions occur. Her narrative, primarily considered as an illness narrative, gives an opportunity to analyse the place of women in journalism as she herself was a reporter that worked for the *New York Post*. She was a competent as well as a confident reporter. However, the pressure that female journalists have to face as compared to the males could be witnessed through her work. The ability of the women journalists are bound to be judged taking into consideration their gender. Instead of prioritising talent, gender takes the front seat while judging work dynamics. As E.A. Bennett notes:

> Is there any sexual reason why a woman should be a less accomplished journalist than a man? I can find none. Admitted that in certain fields – say politics – he will surpass her, are there not other fields in which she is pre-eminent, fields of which the man will not so much as climb the gate? And even in politics women have excelled. (Bennett 2)

The competition that should have been fair between males and females is already corrupted since males are always considered more efficient than the females. From how Cahalan writes about the competition in her field, it is evident of her underlying insecurity. This pressure of excelling affected all females more drastically because not only did they have to compete with fellow journalists, they have to prove their stand as a woman. Men are not pressured by the gender bias as society is highly male dominated. It is the females who are doubly pressured – one coming from the competition in the work place and the other from the gender bias and stereotypes. This pressure not only adds to their physical stress, but also brings with it mental stress. As we read more about Cahalan in her work, it becomes clear how the world of journalism was a catalyst that fed her insecurities, further worsening her growing illness.

Media and journalism not only discriminate women journalists, but they also discriminate women through their representations of women to the world. A report by Jos Heezen titled "Gender Equality in the Media Sector", it was observed that women were likely to not have any major dialogues in advertisements. They are mostly represented as product users rather than figures of authority. Furthermore, they are commodified and presented as objects of admiration. They are also displayed as taking care of children or in other domestic spheres where they act submissive and compassionate. The media objectifies women and promotes a stereotypical image of a perfect woman – using adjectives like "white". "skinny", "blond". The question arises here – who decides that these define a perfect woman? Who decides that only such women are to be called attractive? Cahalan compares herself to the ex-girlfriend of her boyfriend and feels insecure since she had "bony hips", "bleached blond" hair, and looked, what Cahalan considers. "attractive". However, while defining herself, she uses adjectives like having "wild" hair and her face "distorted and unfamiliar". These comparisons are based on the images presented of the "perfect woman" by the media. Thus, her words represent the insecurities that millions of women suffer from due to the stereotypes promoted by the world of media and journalism. The comparisons make Cahalan feel more insecure about herself, further increasing her fragile mental condition arise from the idea of beauty that the media wrongly presents to the world. This image is promoted to suit the interests of the male dominated society and the politics of patriarchy. "Insecurity is a part of the job" – this is something Cahalan tells herself to create a false sense of power and strength.

This work pressure in the world of journalism is common. But this pressure is doubled for women, and Cahalan is a true example. Even though she is a confident person, we see how she easily accepts the doctor's hypothesis that perhaps she has bipolar disorder. It would seem she too is subconsciously accepting the patriarchal bias against woman. Perhaps if she had more confidence and had been free of this bias laid on woman, she too would be able to question the claims laid on her intellect and capabilities. It is her brother who stands up for her and refuses to believe that she is suffering from any sort of depression or bipolar disorder. This insecurity that lies in women due to the unequal treatment from the patriarchal society is thus, worsened by the media. The image of an "ideal" woman that the patriarchal society wants is promoted at the expense of the true woman who is equally intelligent and capable as the males.

It is this pressure to prove themselves to the society that often leads women to deny their femininity, their uniqueness. However, by denying femininity, women empowerment cannot be achieved. We see Cahalan trying to be display "boldness" and "competitiveness" like many other women. However, it mentally, it does not help her and her condition only takes a turn towards the worse. Furthermore, as Susannah tries her hardest not to fall victim to lose herself, we realise how she is doubly marginalised. Firstly, she is a woman in a profession that is male dominated. This pressure to be equal to the males is a constant insecurity that exists in women in this profession like herself. Secondly, she is a victim of an illness which would further make people question if she would ever be able to be "normal" again after her recovery from her neurological disease. "That's not the Susannah I know", said a male colleague of Cahalan. He was doubtful whether Cahalan would be able to function actively and efficiently like before. Cahalan who already had a fragile confidence, further felt hurt hearing such remarks from the male colleagues. Perhaps he would not be so harsh in his judgment had it been a male since men are conditioned to think that women are more sensitive and sensuous. Hence, he sees her as more vulnerable. There is more pity, rather than sympathy for female victims, be it any profession. Furthermore, the concept of "normal" and "insanity" itself is questionable. This label is also a social construct, which again is fitted to suit the standards of those in power.

In the past, women who acted submissive and remained confined to domestic work were considered "angel of the house", while those who expressed their passions freely and rebelled were put in asylums, with them being termed "mad" or as "monsters". Even in the modern society, these biases exist but in different disguises. For instance, the media promoting the image of "perfect" woman is a way of trying to condition the society into thinking and acting according to the interests of the patriarchal society. Just as women did not get many opportunities in the past, they are still not given equal treatment. Journalism is the profession where women training for it are more, but only few get equally acknowledged as compared to men. Thus, although times and techniques have changed, the discrimination and stereotypes still exist against women. Therefore, to change the mindsets of people, the best solution could be brought through the help of the media and literature. Both of them have the access to the world and could reach the masses. With the help of journalism and literature, the people in the world could question the existing norms and would be forced to think from a different perspective. It would also encourage women to come forth and be more vocal about their discrimination and problems. This way, the world could perhaps hope for a future where the opportunities for both men and women would be equal. They would be judged based on their capabilities and talents, rather than based on their gender.

Works Cited

Cahalan, Susannah. *Brain on Fire: My Month of Madness*. Penguin Books, 2012.

Beauvoir, Simone de. *The Second Sex*. Vintage Classics, 2015.www.sfu.ca/~decaste/OISE/page2

/files/deBeauvoirIntro.pdf. Accessed on 2 Apr. 2020.

Bennett, Enoch Arnold. *Journalism for Women*. Project Gutenburg-tm Ebooks, 8 Sept. 2014.

www.gutenberg.org/cache/epub/8405/pg8405.txt. Accessed on 21 Oct. 2020.

Byerly, Carolyn M.. *Global Report on the Status of Women in the News Media*. International Women's Media Foundation, 2011. https://www.iwmf.org/wp-content/uploads/2018/06/IWMF-Global-Report.pdf Accessed on 3 Apr, 2022.

Franz, Suzanne. *Women and Journalism*. I.B. Tauris, 2019. https//reutersinstitute.politic.ox.ac.uk/sites/default/files/research/files/Women%2520and%2520Journalism.pdf. Accessed on 21 Oct. 2020. Accessed on 1Oct. 2020.

Geertsema, M. "Women and News: Making Connections between the Global and the Local". *Feminist Media Studies*, vol. 9(2), 2009, pp. 149-172. https//core.ac.uk/download/pdf/62428584.pdf. Accessed on 5Oct. 2020.

McCracken, Katie, Dr. Ana FitzSimons, Dr. Sarah Priest, Sylvia Girstmair and Brenda Murphy. *GenderEquality and in the Media Sector*. Policy Department for Citizen's Rights and Constitutional Affairs, 2018. https://www.europarl.europa.eu/RegData/etudes/STUD/2018/596839/IPOL_STU(2018)596839_EN.pdf Accessed on 14 Mar, 2022.

Shivkumar, I. "Women and Journalism: Commitment and Challenges". *Indian Journal ofWomen Studies*, vol XI, 2018. https://www.researchgate.net/publication/347910318 Accessed on 1 Jan, 2021.

Woolf, Virginia. *A Room of One's Own*. Hogarth Press, 1929. https://maulanaazadcollegekolkata.ac.in/pdf/open-resources/A-Room-of-Ones-Own-Virginia-Woolf-PDF.pdf.Accessed on 21 Sept. 2021.

CHAPTER 15

Food Politics and Female Autonomy: The Difficulty of Making Choices in Han Kang's *The Vegetarian*

Dr. Nivedita Gupta

Abstract

Han Kang's novel *The Vegetarian* has brought to attention more subtle forms of violence embedded in social and cultural practices in South Korea. Discourses around eating and dining were always thought to be gender-neutral and feminist analyses only restricted itself to question cooking as a gendered phenomenon as it was believed to be the primary cause of women's removal from the political sphere. However, food consumption and dining laws also determine female consciousness as is evident in Kang's novel. The narrative highlights how deeply the success of masculinist institutions have distorted human relationship with nature so that returning to the fundamental state of existence is tantamount to suicide. The present research paper on *The Vegetarian* firstly, examines food as a gendered cultural discourse that supports continual subordination of women, ecology, and animals. Vegetarian feminism as an offshoot of ecofeminism explores how eating and dining practices are gendered and sexualised and often legitimise direct and/or indirect forms of violence against women and animals. Second, the paper shows how women's everyday choices are often viewed as dangerous if these do not comply with the traditional nature of gender roles and activities. When the protagonist, Yeong-Hye, rejects meat, clothes, social gatherings, and all forms of domestic obedience, she threatens the very fabric of South Korean society that maintains a hierarchical relationship between men and women whereby men are the disciplinarians and women the ones to be disciplined. Men in the novel are the aggressors. Violence and cruelty are their cultural assets, and they use their culturally legitimised power freely against women and animals. This analysis includes a discussion on Confucianism as a popular South Korean philosophy that advocates sexual division of labor, roles, and rights. At last, the paper also argues that in the novel's title, the word 'vegetarian' does not imply a support for vegetarianism as an eating practice but in this context, vegetarianism implies women's attempt to return to nature which symbolises a return to her natural primal self where she can accept her body, sexuality and voice as they are; abandon all social constructs and identity markers; and reclaim her space in nature.

Keywords: South Korean women's movements, ecofeminism, female agency, Confucianism

Article

Ecofeminism as an offshoot of eco-criticism often questions the patriarchal nature of various institutions that place unwarranted value on capitalist principles of personal ownership and individualism over the primal instinct of life. Ecofeminism goes by the belief that patriarchy was bolstered by the rise and expansion of capitalism which resulted in the creation of discourses and institutions that favored men over women, culture over religion, personal self over the other and the rational over the emotional. Imperialism and colonialism succeeded because of the same conviction that those who are cultured also bear the white man's burden of saving the rest who live in the jungles. Research shows how colonial practices were highly gendered with native lands been often imagined as female bodies to be conquered and possessed; and native men as effeminate and unworthy of protecting their own lands and women.

While studying the history and culture of developing and/or underdeveloped countries like South Korea, it is important to make an analysis that begins by questioning the gendered nature of emerging popular trends in these countries including urbanisation, development, and capitalism to uncover the deep links between the exploitation of nature and women. Ecofeminism does not only draw upon feminist concerns but by that virtue also includes discussions on socialism and various other justice movements like animal liberation movement, environmentalism, and anti-nuclear activism.

Han Kang is a South Korean writer who won the Man Booker International Prize in fiction in 2016 for her novel, *The Vegetarian*, first published in 2007 which was inspired by her short story, 'The Fruit of My Women'. Originally written in South Korean, *The Vegetarian* was translated into English by Deborah Smith. *The Vegetarian* is a three-part novel set in modern-day Seoul that recounts the story of a graphic artist and a married woman. Yeong-Hye, the protagonist, disturbs her world of pretended marital bliss when one day she suddenly decides not to ever consume meat again after an epiphanous nightmare that makes her see the act of violence embedded in seemingly simple human practices like eating. Her humble decision of turning vegetarian begins a tragic gender struggle inside her home with devastating consequences for her. Yeong-Hye's story then takes the form of a prolonged female quest for greater autonomy over her voice, body, and visibility as she decides to fight resolutely against social norms demanding unwarranted obedience and submission from her. In the novel, the choice of turning vegetarian can be read as an act of rebellion for two reasons: Firstly, Yeong-Hye's decision to turn vegetarian goes against the most widely accepted norm of eating meat in South Korea and reveals Yeong-Hye's acute urge to be independent as against tradition that cannot allow women to take independent decisions; second, her decision could also amount to be a possible threat to patriarchal forces of capitalism and consumption if women begin to reclaim their primal links to nature as Yeong-Hye does when she sees herself as an extension of the natural world. Subsequent humiliation faced by Yeong-Hye reveals how important conformity and performance are for society and that is also why *The Vegetarian* becomes an evocative tale of female agency. The three parts of the novel are titled – The Vegetarian, The Mongolian Mark and The Flaming Tree, which lead to metamorphosis in Yeong-Hye but the kind that fails to show a conclusive result. Her quest for identity and self-affirmation becomes muddled because of patriarchal bondage, filial conflict, domestic abuse and a normalisation of cruelty in her society.

The present research paper firstly examines 'carno-phallogocentricism' as a gendered discourse that supports continual subordination of women, ecology, and animals (Malatino131). This includes a brief discussion on Vegetarian feminism which explores how eating and dining practices are gendered and sexualised and often legitimise direct and/or indirect forms of violence against women and animals. Social expectation that women must maintain their feminine delicacy by avoiding meat alcohol while men must freely experiment with food reveals how masculinist ideology has determined gender difference for so long. Second, it reveals how women's ordinary everyday choices come to be seen as dangerous if these do not comply with the traditional nature of gender roles and activities. When Yeong-Hye rejects meat, clothes, social gatherings, domestic duties, and all forms of compliance, she threatens the very fabric of South Korean society that places too much emphasis on male desire and discipline that must be maintained by violence and cruelty towards the one seen as powerless. The men in the novel are the aggressors; the ones who also control the narratorial voice in the novel with Yeong-Hye's sister taking on the narration briefly in one out of the three parts of the novel. However, Yeong-Hye's sister only acts as the custodian of patriarchy as her voice leads to further silencing of Yeong-Hye, the other, who is often described as absurd, unsound and dangerous. This analysis includes a discussion on Confucianism as a philosophy popular in South Korea that advocates sexual division of labor, roles, and rights. At last, the paper also argues that in Han Kang's novel, *The Vegetarian*, the word 'vegetarian' does not imply a support for vegetarianism as an eating practice but in this context, vegetarianism implies women's attempt to return to nature which symbolises a return to her natural primal self where she can accept her body, sexuality and voice as they are; abandon all social constructs and identity markers; and reclaim her space in nature.

Confucianism and Female Resistance

South Korean women's movements have neither been well-documented by the Western critics nor been acknowledged by the South Korean political, social, and historical analysts. South Korean women's movements began in the nineteenth century under Japanese colonial rule but remained overshadowed because of rapid economic, social, and political changes orchestrated by foreign rule. Many of these movements were motivated and limited by socialist concerns as they aimed to only provide rehabilitation to women. Women's movements were expected to prioritise national liberation and actively contribute to the re-unification of Korean society (Jung 1). Starting in 1980's, women did begin to mobilise around the issue of sexual violence but political instability and imperial violence always remained more pressing issues. Since then, women's movements in South Korea have continued to be shaped and impacted by the political contexts and, with time, the issues and concerns of women's movements have widened (Song Woo – Hur 181). However, the idea of an independent women has never received much warrant amongst South Korean patriarchal bloc.

The Vegetarian by Han Kang is a persistent exploration of cruelty embedded in human civilisational practices against both nature and women. As mentioned earlier, *The Vegetarian* is a novel narrated in three parts with each part showing the gradual retreat of Yeong-Hye into an unknown wilderness of human existence. The narrative is never fully owned by Yeong-Hye just as her life never was. The entire narration is seemingly owned by three characters, the first being her aggressive husband, Mr. Cheong, who tells Yeong-Hye's story in first-person narrative. Second, in the third-person narrative is Yeong-Hye's unnamed brother-in-law who is a video artist and is sexually attracted to Yeong-Hye. Finally, the third narratorial voice is of Yeong-Hye's sister, In-Hye, who despite all her primal urges decides to conform. Her own voice is mostly muted only finding expression in nightmares and dreams. Yeong-Hye's gradual and obsessive insistence on becoming a tree underlines her resistance against panoptical male gaze that fetishizes and restricts women, thus, resulting in feeling of self-loathing and self-denial in them. Someone who was always known to be submissive and obedient, Yeong-Hye's silent protest unleashes a tempest of male anger. In Part 1, when Yeong-Hye announces that she will no longer eat meat, her husband is shocked at her non-conformism but also, for the first time, feels intrigued by her defiance. Her father's disgust with her decision is more provocative as he first slaps her and then asks her husband and brother to hold her while the meat is pushed down her throat. This kind of violence is accepted as both a norm and a necessity whenever women seem to transgress their divinely ordained duties. The story reveals how Yeong-Hye had been continually subjected to her father's abuse under the pretext of discipline and order as she was growing up. Both the sisters seemingly know that female disobedience is a punishable offence and a threat to patriarchy. Quite interestingly, Yeong-Hye's cruel mistreatment is equated with the continual exploitation of animals and nature. She has a recurring dream where she sees blood dripping meat and her hands soaked in blood as a proof of her being a murderer. It is this dream that forces her to take the life-altering decision. However, the nightmare has deeper connotation. It is argued that the nightmare also forces Yeong-Hye to reflect on her own position in her household. Th bizarre and grotesque details described in the scene of the nightmare might, on the superficial level, make one think that Yeong-Hye has turned mad as is proven by her decision to turn vegetarian and then eventually abandon all forms of eating altogether, but on deeper reading, one feels that her rebellion against eating meat is informed by the realisation that meat consumption and domesticity are patriarchal acts of domination. Both women and animals become objectified as mere means to support male power and authority. Yeong-Hye realises that she needs to rebel even at the cost of an evident loss of sanity.

Whereas in Part 1, Yeong-Hye's decision to turn vegetarian suddenly makes her visible to her husband who otherwise believed her to be quite unremarkable, timid, sickly thin and unattractive, in Part 2, it is the discovery of the "Mongolian Mark" on her body that goes on to intrigue the unnamed brother-in-law, a video artist. A blue birth mark common to people of Asian descent, a Mongolian Mark often disappears when people turn five or before puberty. It is seen as a blessing of a higher power or a sign of a pre-life when a child is blessed by her ancestors. In-Hye's husband's inquisitiveness turns into a sexual obsession as the image of the mark on Yeong-Hye's buttocks begins to inspire him to find unconventional and new ways to express himself through art. It is his own obsession with the plant kingdom as an artist that gets reinforced by the bizarreness of Yeong-Hye's mental condition. This episode also reveals the phallogocentric nature of digital art where men are the artists and women become their muted sexual objects-subjects meant to support their artistic ambitions by becoming objects of male fascination. The brother-in-law shoots a video of Yeong-Hye's bare body, paints flowers all over her and engages her in a sexual orgy with another man before finally raping her. His panoptical artistic imagination and creative energies know nothing but how to consume, control and own his art.

Often confused with religion, Confucianism remains the foundation of Korean culture and faith. With the decline of Buddhism caused by the degeneracy of the institute in South Korea, Confucianism increasingly became a major school of thought. Kumari Jayawardena, in her seminal book, Feminism and Nationalism in The Third World, discusses the powerful impact of Confucianism on women's culture in South Korea. She argues that Confucianism led to rigid stratification of gender roles as social institutions began to be masculinized while women became confined into domesticity. With a few privileges accorded, the overall discourse mandated an absolute control over women to the extent that women did not even have names; they were known by their husband's names (Jayawardena 247). Jayawardena also discusses the architectural/spatial violence that women were subjected to. While men socialised in open spaces as if the world was naturally theirs to own, women were confined into inner parts of the home and were not permitted to be socially visible. Women's inclusion in South Korea has ever since remained difficult and slow also proven by the slow success of its feminist movements. As an alternative to Buddhist emphasis on vegetarianism much professed by Chinese Buddhists, Confucianism does not stigmatize meat-eating. Rather, Confucianism authorises meat-eating. Gradually, with political upheavals and processes of national reconstruction, veganism came to be viewed as a sin. Processes of identity formation especially during nationalist movements usually demand undivided faith in historical and cultural practices and thus social and national identities are forged. Confucianism propagated a strict disciplinary compliance often viewed as the only means to fight against foreign infiltration. Women's culture, therefore, had to be more strongly controlled and regulated as women are the reproducers of a community. Confucianism also believes that women's bodies are corporeal while men's bodies have the ability to transcend their bodily limitation and achieve great heights. The men in, *The Vegetarian,* are deeply invested in this parochial ideology and seem to find strength and legitimacy through it. In their imagination, a woman is a fossilized and static entity whose only performative act is to obey and conform. Male domination has been explored in the novel through different characters such as Yeong-Hye's father whose lust for domestic control makes him abusive towards both women and animals; Yeong-Hye's husband who finds his wife unremarkable because she does not fit the social construct of a beautiful woman; and her brother-in-law's voyeuristic gaze resulting in sexual assault are all representative acts of everyday violence that women bear only because these acts get justified by tradition.

Eventually, Yeong-Hye's growing conflation between self and the natural world makes her abandon food completely. While fighting against male oppression, she rejects all forms of consumerism. As the novel progresses so does Yeong-Hye's association with the vegetal world; she wishes to survive on sunlight and water. This, obviously, affects her psychologically and physically but it can be read as Yeong-Hye's absolute rejection of toxic masculinity that reinforces structural inequalities and systematic violence against women and nature. By this time, the reader realises that Yeong-Hye's evolution/dissolution may begin with her forging links with herself and the animals but ends up in her seeing herself as a vegetation. Han Kang writes about a conversation between Yeong-Hye and In-Hye:

> "They say my insides have all atrophied, you know." In-Hye was lost for words. Yeong-Hye moved her emaciated face closer to her sister. "I'm not an animal anymore, sister," she said, first scanning the empty ward as if about to disclose a momentous secret. "I don't need to eat, not now. I can live without it. All I need is sunlight."
>
> "What are you talking about? Do you really think you've turned into a tree? How could a plant talk? How can you think these things?"" (Han & Smith, 2015, p.153-154),

There is no way that her struggle will be understood by her sister who is more of a conformist. She sees and questions discrimination but does not have enough strength or madness in her to register dissent. Despite knowing everything about Yeong-Hye's childhood trauma, she becomes complicit as Yeong-Hye is continually represented as a mad woman.

Yeong-Hye refuses to be domesticated and disciplined and meat only becomes for her a tool of resistance. Through her dietary opposition, Yeong-Hye tries to fight against female disenfranchisement so acutely visible in the foundations of all social, political and economic discourses. It is just not the men who fail to show compassion but also women who learnt obedience and advocate it as a woman's natural duty.

In the third part, *Flaming Trees*, In-Hye narrates her sister's current condition suggesting that Yeong-Hye's insanity has grown to a dangerous level. According to Yeong-Hye, becoming a plant – part of nature was her only recourse to decry violence. It is obvious by now that she associates violence with patriarchy and consumerism. Yeong-Hye's attempt to dehumanise herself unfolds a serious problem that humans face – it shows how deeply human laws have altered the natural world and how it has become almost impossible for humans to reclaim their true place in the natural order of things. Yeong-Hye's story revolves around her isolation from the patriarchal society until she discovers a safe place for herself in nature. Her vehement opposition against patriarchy is rooted in her childhood memories of her father who first introduced her to gender binary of the powerful and the powerless. Very soon, she realises that binaries determine all human relations including man's relationship with nature.

Conclusion

Feminism has always invested itself in guaranteeing women equal rights with men. Western feminism has often been denounced for its maternalistic attitude towards third world feminism as it has only proved to work on colonial prejudice against the natives, particularly, native women. South Korean feminist movements have tried to create a niche by professing different goals and feminist concerns for themselves. Han Kang's The Vegetarian opens a powerful discussion on the current success of Western capitalism that began by first, destroying the indigenous ways in which the natives lived, and now has leaked into all societies to advocate a culture that supports disproportionate consumerism, commodification, and accumulation. The ones who suffer in the greed to own are often women and nature, both of which are assumed to weak, needy and meant to be possessed. The Vegetarian shows a woman's absolute rejection of the formulaic ways in which we are meant to spend our lives – obeying, fitting-in and being socially acceptable. The book is a feminist narrative and shares many common characteristics with feminist works, one that could not be mentioned earlier because of the limited scope of the paper is, madness. In many earlier works, women writers have often imagined a rebellious woman as someone right on the verge of madness as that is what women demanding autonomy become in the eyes of society. Yeong-Hye's madness is not so much a result of her decline as it is a consequence of people's inability to understand what she wants. The violence she is subjected to right after her announcement of turning vegan also leads her to feel de-humanised. It, quite obviously, results in her disengagement from human laws and existence. Consequently, she begins to associate herself with nature as a means to belong and be accepted. The madness is the result of patriarchal humiliation than of mental delusion, though delusion and schizophrenia are bound to eventually set in.

Works Cited

Bright, Shilpa. "An Ecofeminist Reading of Han Kang's The Vegetarian." *Smart Moves Journal IJELLH*, vol.9, no. 5, 2021.

Casey, Rose. "Willed Arboreality: Feminist Worldmaking in Han Kang's The Vegetarian." *Critique: Studies in Contemporary Fiction*, vol. 62, no. 3, 2020, pp. 347-360, DOI: 10.1080/00111619.2020.1841725.

Cassell, Eric J. *The Nature of Suffering and the Goals of Medicine.* Oxford University Press, 1991.

Chen, Chao-Ju. "The Difference that Differences Make: Asian Feminism and the Politics of Difference." *Asian Journal of Women's Studies*, vol. 13, no. 3, 2007, pp. 7-36. JSTOR, DOI: 10.1080/12259276.2007.11666028.

Choudhary, Jharna. "The Struggle with Disease Taxonomy in Han Kang's The Vegetarian," *Rupkatha Journal on Interdisciplinary Studies in Humanities*, vol. 12:6, 2020. DOI: 10.21659/rupkatha.v1n6.03.

Elfving-Hwang, Joanna. *Representations of Femininity in Contemporary South Korean Women's Literature.* London: Global Oriental, 2010. Print.

Felman, Shoshana. "Women and Madness: The Critical Phallacy." *Diacritics*, 5:4, 1975, pp. 2–10, www.jstor.org/stable/464958. Accessed 17 June. 2022.

Hur, Song-Woo. "Mapping South Korean Women's Movements during and after Democratisation: Shifting Identities." *East Asian Social Movements*, 2010, pp. 181–203., DOI:10.1007/978-0-387-09626-1_9.

Jung, Kyungja. *Practicing Feminism in South Korea.* USA and Canada: Routledge, 2014. Print.

Kang, Han. *The Vegetarian. Translated by Deborah Smith*, Portobello Books, 2015.

Kim, Won-Chung. "Eating and Suffering in Han Kang's The Vegetarian." *CLCWeb: Comparative Literature and Culture,* vol. 21, no. 5, 2019. DOI:10.7771/1481-4374.3390.

Kumari, Jayawardena. *Feminism and Nationalism in The Third World.* London and NY: Verso P, 2016. Print

Malatino, Hilary. "Carnophallogocentricism and The Sexual Politics of Meat." *Journal for Critical Animal Studies*, vol. 9, no. 3, 2011, pp.128-34.

Narayan, Uma. "Undoing the 'Package Picture' of Cultures." *Signs: Journal of Women in Culture and Society*, vol. 25, no. 4, 2000, pp. 1083–1086. JSTOR, www.jstor.org/stable/3175491. Accessed 17 June. 2022.

Showalter, Elaine. *The Female Malady: Women, Madness, and English Culture*, 1830-1980. Penguin Books, 1987.

CHAPTER 16

Partition and Women Writers: A Study

Dr. Gurpreet Kour

Abstract

The purpose of this Chapter is to examine a few fictional works on Partition created by women writers, with a focus on how women's perspectives are told against the backdrop of Partition. Its purpose is to bring the experience of women during Partition to the forefront of the study and to shatter the silence caused by dominant narratives that have consistently ignored the subject. This study aims to uncover women's "little histories" and "discover" women in Partition as depicted in women's literature. Rather than a total rewrite of extant history, a re-angle of our lens is required to bring into focus those histories that have never been documented, rather than a total rewrite of available history. The history of women is an example of this.

The goal of the study is to demonstrate that women writers do not describe women's experiences of Partition in isolation, but rather incorporate elements of everyday life into their depictions of Partition. The most common feature of the women's fiction examined in this paper is that it is not solely focused with narrativising women's experiences during Partition. They weave this framework with the story of women's experiences as women. The goal of the paper is to present a more nuanced image of the truth of an event that is commonly depicted in black and white but has many shades in the perspective of female writers.

Keywords: Partition, women writers, literature, history, isolation

> There are certain images from my past which have always haunted me. Partition was a very violent experience for everybody in the Punjab. Although I was very young then, I saw chance killings, fires, dead bodies. There are images which have stayed with me. These were also the stories I grew up with. – Bapsi Sidhwa, "*My Place in the World*"

When the Indian subcontinent was separated into two countries, India and Pakistan, it was one of the most heinous events in the country's history. It is also one of the world's largest migrations in history.

Some of us have heard many stories of Partition from our ancestors, or have seen movies or read books about it, and even three generations later, discussion of Partition may still send shivers down the spine. Thousands of individuals migrated in both directions, and thousands more were never able to arrive because long-coexisting tribes started attacking one another. As a result of division, over a million people have died and fifteen million more were displaced. Women have been abducted and sexually assaulted. They were also assassinated by their own family in order to safeguard their honour from future rape and abduction.

Many accounts of Partition have been written and portrayed in books, documentaries, and documentaries. Books about the Partition, especially those published by those who experienced through it, or by others to whom they have related their stories, or even by Partition historians, are an invaluable source of information. Partition is made available to future generations through these publications, as well as films and movies on the issue.

The partition of India and the accompanying horrible riots inspired many brilliant minds in India and Pakistan to create literary and cinematic depictions of the event. While some works concentrated on the horrors committed during the refugee migration, others centered on the aftermath of the division and the difficulties faced by refugees on both sides of the border. Literature and cinema based on actual story of the divide are still being produced more than 60 years after the split.

The human cost of independence and partition is depicted in works such as Khushwant Singh's Train to Pakistan (1956), several short stories by Saadat Hassan Manto, Urdu poems by Faiz Ahmad Faiz, Bhisham Sahni's Tamas (1974), Manohar Malgonkar's A Bend in the Ganges (1965), and Bapsi Sidhwa's Ice-Candy Man (1988), among others. Salman Rushdie's novel Midnight's Children (1980), which won the Booker Prize and the Booker of Bookers, describes the tale of children born with magical abilities on August 14, 1947, at 12 a.m.

The long campaign for India's independence from the British Raj, which began with the 1857 Indian Mutiny, gained traction after World War II. However, India's desire for self-rule was accompanied with severe inter-communal violence. The Indian National Congress and the Muslim League were unable to harmonise their viewpoints, thereby exacerbating the chaos and sectarianism that erupted. As a result, India was partitioned into three independent nation-states after the British left in 1947. As a result of this decision, millions of people were forced to quit their homes and relocate to the other state, slogging through corpse-strewn landscapes and uncertain futures.

They could never have predicted that this political choice, which had nothing to do with their own safety, would turn out to be one of the deadliest man-made tragedies in history. Houses were demolished and looted. A shower of bloated and misshapen carcasses hindered the flow of water through canals. Thousands of people have died as a result of ethnic violence.

Even if they made it to the other side, they had a hard time finding peace. Makeshift refugee camps serve as breeding grounds for a wide range of diseases. The tragedy that followed Partition has left an indelible mark on India's history.

The anniversary of the partition of India and Pakistan has been marked many times throughout history. These histories have been rewritten and moulded to match state narratives as political turmoil have risen and decreased. As history typically is, the stories that arise from partition are usually emotional. The goal is to elicit a response. A moving reminder of the pain people go through in the hopes of a better future. They're also strictly controlled. Different accounts of the same incident can be found in textbooks on both sides of the border. Many perspectives and stories have been marginalised despite efforts to bridge the divide.

These lost tales typically include women from the subcontinent. There have been recent initiatives to draw attention to the traumas that many women have experienced. Despite this, the plot is heavily skewed toward men. On our platform, authors have taken it upon themselves to share their stories. Even fiction can give us a deep, heartfelt understanding into stories we'd almost forgotten about.

The majority of stories about women in prison focus on the sexual assault they experienced. The spotlight is still on the males who perpetrated the crimes the majority of the time. Female authors, on the other hand, give this woman a voice, completely changing the story. By looking at two of my favourite books on division from both sides of the border, I'd like to highlight why two of my favourite novels on partition from both sides of the border are so significant for the narrative they tell.

The Women's Courtyard by Khadija Mastur, Translated by Daisy Rockwell

Mastur tells the narrative of a Muslim family in the years leading up to and following partition. The plot centres around Aliya, a young child, and her observations of life inside the house. The story is narrated from Aliya's point of view, with emphasis on other female household members, including Aliya's mother, Tehmina, her friend Chammi, and Kusum. The women spent much of their time in the house's courtyard, as the title suggests, and Mastur analyses the unusual ways in which women were active in the politics of the time by restricting the narrative to that courtyard.

That isn't to say that life does not exist outside of the courtyard. That's not to imply there's no life beyond the courtyard. The Women's Courtyard offers a variety of viewpoints on how it affected women at the period and how it forced them to modify and compromise on many levels. The novel is a critique of patriarchy, which is rooted in society and even in the movement, rather than of the movement itself. While it is necessary to fight for one's nation, as the men in Aliya's family do, they are torn between their duties as breadwinners and freedom fighters, illustrating the pressures they experienced from their families and society. The scene of the home in the novel and the Aangan, on the other hand, forces the reader to consider a typically female occupied area and how their world is constrained by it. While the men are out fighting for independence and discussing it in the drawing salons, the ladies are never given access to this realm. Even while it impacts them in other ways, such as psychological and economic, the feminine gaze does not infringe on that domain. Aliya is the only one seen learning about the movement from her Uncle, who encourages her to do so. The story depicts various gender expectations that were in place at the time and are still in place today, when women are not allowed to vote.

Aliya is well ensconced within the claustrophobic constraints of her home, largely sheltered from the woes of a world in upheaval as the final phase of India's war for independence play out and Partition looms. But she is blocked off from the outside world, with all of its unlimited possibilities for those who dream of self-sufficiency, and is left to keep her dreams alive amidst her extended family's broken dreams and wreckage of clashing ideas.

The safe haven she has grown up in is insufficient to protect her from the trauma of losing her adored elder sister Tehmina and dear friend Kusum to suicide when they place too much faith in the possibility of intoxicating love and romance in the otherwise landscape of their lives, only to be left heartbroken. These events have left her with no trust in romance, especially because she has also witnessed her mother and aunt's weddings to men who are more committed to their politics. Aliya is frightened by her mother's rage and pettiness, as well as her aunt's emotional wreckage. She is filled with empathy, has a wellspring of good sense, and never stops caring for her tortured loved ones, preferring to learn from the experience while teaching herself to insulate herself from the pain produced by irreversibly terrible judgement.

Men who are connected by family seem to have unrestricted access and are given an unusually free hand to flirt, stalk, molest, or exploit their cousins in this cloistered zone, which is intended for women. There's Safdar, who adores Tehmina, Shakeel, who has no qualms about robbing his relatives, and Jameel, who won't take no for an explanation. Despite a certain attraction, Aliya is adamant in her rejection of Jameel's love for her, fully aware that he has mistreated another cousin Chammi, writes mediocre poetry, hasn't differentiated himself in the professional sphere, and is a little too much like some other men in her life who sacrifice their women and children on the shrine of their politics.

Aliya leaves home frequently as a student and then as a teacher. When she returns to the 'safety' of her home, the story pauses, but it resumes when she returns. Mastur places women in the partition story in a significant way. However, there is a psychological and emotional cost. Family relationships begin to deteriorate as each family member delves further into their own political ideas. Chammi becomes entangled in the politics that are engulfing the globe around her, disregarding her family's boundaries.

Aliya's story, as well as the stories of the women she refers to as her family, differs from the standard partition story. It does, however, shed light on how the incident impacted so many families and lives. As Aliya is compelled to go with her mother, the boundaries built between Aliya and Chammi rip them apart.

The novel is groundbreaking in that it introduces us to a heroine who is determined in her opposition to patriarchy, even when enforcers tempt her with the chance of love and marriage, both of which Aliya recognises are more likely to entrap her than the constraints she has been fighting her entire life. Mastur doesn't hold back when it comes to women that enable sexism. Aliya's mother is an especially heartbreaking example of a gender imposter. A beautiful book that illustrates the difficult conflicts that women face away from the battlefield. Mastur's art contrasts sharply with Shauna Singh Baldwin's 'What the Body Remembers', which illustrates a different facet of the region's sad past scars.

What the Body Remembers By Shauna Singh Baldwin

Baldwin narrates the story of Roop, a little Sikh girl living on the other side of the world in what is now Pakistan. Roop understands what is expected of a lady as she matures. As the young second wife of a much older Sikh businessman, she is thrust into a world she is unfamiliar with. When seen through Roop's innocent eyes, the story of Khalistan and the notion of Sikh sovereignty take on a whole new meaning.

Baldwin deftly navigates the changing times. Roop grew up in a diverse neighbourhood, where her best friend was a young Muslim girl. When tensions rise and her father shifts his tone to fight for the Sikh religion's integrity, Roop realises how delicate these relationships are. Years later, Roop re-encounters a childhood acquaintance in a totally different context. Both have realised that their bond will never be good enough to withstand the rifts that threaten to split their world apart. Sardarji is progressively preoccupied by the uproar over freedom and the future of the Indian state as Roop, taught to use traditional feminine wiles, battles for his favour and the children Roop soon produces. Baldwin succeeds on two levels: she captures the shifting political and religious emergence of world India and Pakistan while also exploring Roop's dramatic metamorphosis from a haughty, self-centered girl to a caring wife and mother who has become the family's backbone.

What the Body Remembers, despite its differences, has a lot of common ground with Mastur's novel. Roop, like Aliya, has no choice but to cross the border. She, like Aliya, has no say in whether or not she must comply. Roop, on the other hand, is taking a detour. Roop is struggling to stay alive on the train, wondering if she will ever meet her husband again, whereas Aliya has the leisure of flying.

Kusum, her sister-in-law, does not have the same luck. During a house raid, Kusum is tortured and murdered. In an act of vengeance against all woman kinds, Kusum's womb is attacked. We see how many distinct stories develop from the same event in three ladies from two different houses. How each individual has their own set of scars to bear, each one different.

Conclusion

On the surface, the two novels have nothing in common. Privilege, class, religion, and country are all separate, if not diametrically opposed, concepts. But that is precisely what connects them. Aside their differences, both compositions are centered on stories of women as individuals. This distinction has been obliterated by state partition narratives. Yet it is precisely because of this uniqueness that we appreciate the importance of all those who took part in the struggle of 1947, and that we need to know deeper about them than the numbers and statistics provided to us.

Work cited

Baldwin, S.S. What The Body Remembers. New York: Anchor, 2001. Print.

Mastur, Khadija. *The Women's Courtyard. Rockwell, Daisy*. Penguin Books, 2018. Print

https://bookriot.com/a-womans-history-of-partition-life-loss-and-identity/

https://www.womensweb.in/2018/05/books-on-partition-women-authors-may18wk3/

https://www.researchgate.net/publication/262843169_Partition_and_Indian_Literature

https://bookriot.com/partition-literature/

https://en.wikipedia.org/wiki/The_1947_Partition_Archive

https://en.wikipedia.org/wiki/Artistic_depictions_of_the_partition_of_India

https://Literariness.org-Gender-Memory-Trauma-Womens-Novels-On-The-Partition-Of-India.

https://mediaindia.eu/culture/amrita-pritam-feminism

https://theseer.in/khadija-masturs-the-womens-courtyard/

https://www.newindianexpress.com/lifestyle/books/2018/nov/11/khadija-masturs-the-womens-courtyard-a-bonafide-feminist-classic-1895630.html

CHAPTER 17

Journey from a Widow to a Father

Hina Koser and *Hiba Khan*

Abstract

Through the short story, *'Widow'*, Gudipati Venkata Chalam has made us aware of the hardships that come in the life of a young (under aged) Widow. Child Marriage was a major societal evil that remained prevailing for a very extended period in India. In 'Widow' we come across the protagonist and narrator of the story who is actually a reflection of how Chalam himself wished the women of his day (and forever) to be. The story leaves a very strong impact on the mind of the reader, pondering upon the difficulties of the life of a Child-Widow. Though it is a fictional story, Chalam has kept it as close to reality as possible because the incidents, no matter how hard to believe they might seem to a 21st century reader, were very real and did actually happen and that's the hard truth. Widows have been a prey to furtive sexual advances of male relatives and reduced to merely an object of scorn and are looked down upon. They have to give up their lifestyle, they undergo a complete change in their way of dressing up. They are punished by society as if they are responsible or desireful for being a Widow. Chalam has penned down these issues with so much realism that a reader cannot help but think and ponder upon the life and miseries of widows and/or child-widows. The story is written from the narrator's perspective and it is almost like the first-hand record of everything that remained unsaid but was existing and slowly eating away at the lives of these women. Such evils have been shown to us by this tremendous literary piece.

Keywords : Child-widow, motherhood, taboo, feminism, fatherhood

Introduction

The story 'Widow' brings out the frustration, anger and uneasiness of a Widow who is also the narrator of the story. This nameless seventeen-year-old widow speaks out how she feels about being a widow in the male-dominated society that puts females below. She points out how her sister-in-law is treated by society just because she has a husband and is also a mother. The narrator notices every minute detail of her sister-in-law. She says that she is cruel towards her child, and says that her (narrator) has more motherhood qualities in her as compared to her sister-in-law but sadly she cannot openly express it because even her touching a child is looked upon as a taboo. The story clearly points out the patriarchy that is deeply instilled in our society.

In the story there is a description of a shawl which was given to the narrator by her then demised father. That shawl was taken away by the sister-in-law because the narrator could not wear it anymore as she was now a widow and she could not use the *fancy* shawl anymore. She only has to wear plain white clothes. Incidents of the shawl symbolise the petty things which a widow is debarred from using in her day-to-day life, here, we, the readers are also aware that this widow is actually a child at heart herself who would like to get nicely dressed and wear fancy clothes, jewellery etc. This child-widow remembers the story of "Cinderella" that her father used to narrate to her. The widows were treated merely as some kind of slaves and their lifestyle used to be changed to that of an animal or maybe even worse in some cases. The narrator states the behavioral discrimination that women go through. When a man's wife passes away, a second wife is ready almost immediately. While on the other hand, when a woman is widowed, she has to suffer immensely as if it was her mistake that her husband died.

Chalam has highlighted that basically in society, a woman's life has value only till the time she is backed by a male (especially a male partner). The narrator says *"how wonderful it used to be when father was alive!"*, she knows that her father would be sad to see her state. Widowed women are looked down on as bad omens. The narrator says that in her religion (Hinduism), Widow re-marriages are a taboo and none thinks about it as if it's a sin for a widow to re-marry. The patriarchal element is evident when the narrator is scared to even hypothetically think of giving birth to a girl child. She says that she should not give birth to a girl child because that way she would eventually only give birth to another widow who would again have to face the same cruelty and the same horrible world that she faces every day of her life. Through her thoughts, the narrator raises the exact same questions that feminism raises in terms of inequality and discrimination. Chalam was an unorthodox writer and philosopher and his writings show a reflection of the woman of his thoughts, who should be bold, strong, stubborn, rebellious and determined.

Gudipati Venkata Chalam as a Writer

Chalam (1894-1979) was a feminist writer, that too, the first Telugu feminist writer. He was a self-proclaimed atheist and had a revolutionary mindset. He wrote about women of his time after closely observing the atrocities that the females went through, laying focus on the physical and the psychological sufferings they faced from the society and even from their own families. He was outspoken and supported women having a say in the fulfilment of their desires and shaping their own destiny. This trait is clearly visible in most of his works and including the short story, *The Widow* too. He wanted these helpless females to rise and revolt against all the behavioural injustice. His themes blended with a specific style and philosophy which made him gain a tremendous place in Telugu literature.

Through the narrator, Chalam has pointed out the intensity of hardships that widowed women go through, and what all must go in the minds of such Child-widows when they face the prominent hypocrisy and unbiased scenarios from the society where a woman with a husband has looked up to while a woman who lost her husband was considered a bad-omen and has to give-away all her basic desires to dress up, have a hair-style, be able to re-marry and start a new life. These widows only had to devote their lives to the memory of their demised husband which is definitely not how the male counterparts who lose their wives, are treated.

> "Why must I alone suffer like this?.. . If because of their karma so many women, without children, are dying out of the sorrow, why don't men to suffer similar karma? The moment one wife is dead, another is ready. Aren't all of us sinners? Perhaps there is a sin exclusive to us."

Here, the narrator speaks the very thoughts of Chalam who tries to understand and makes the readers sympathies with the narrator and other child-widows of the time.

Who is a Father?

Biologically, the father of a child is the parent who sires the baby. Socially, this figure is considered to be a supreme, powerful, responsible and dominant personality. Our society has given unbalanced positions to the parents of a child. The father is generally or ideally the stronger or more powerful one of the two. The child is given the family name of the father and it becomes the identity of the child for life. This way, the father holds somewhat a higher position in the society. The role of the father is to take responsibility of everything which is major in the life of the child. The mother, on the other hand has (stereotypically) been confined to certain duties which are more or less within the four-walls of a household. The mother is not supposed to take up on the duties of the father and vice-versa. This way, the father automatically becomes the socially advanced parent who fights the world and provides for his children and family. This, was the set-up that was prevailing at the time when the short story *The Widow* was written. The deep-rooted patriarchy was obviously the most common thing.

Chalam took a step in changing or rather breaking these gender-roles and made his protagonist take up her miserable life and change it to a story where she becomes the hero and decides to fight the world for her baby. The baby, that she carries in her belly, which was the result of nonconsensual sexual-intercourse. She pushes away the stigma of being a mother who does not have a husband. This kind of rebellion was not acceptable or common for the women of that time and rather could only come from a man.

How a Widow becomes a Father

John Greene said, "The nature of impending fatherhood is that you are doing something that you're unqualified to do, and then you become qualified while doing it". The protagonist (narrator) of the story *Widow* fits in this definition almost perfectly. She was "unqualified" according to the society to be a parent, let alone a father who is regarded a superior figure by the society, but she learns to rise and rebel against the patriarchal society and fight for what she desires. She takes a step to work in the opposite direction of the society. Earlier in the story she is shown as a helpless victim who suffers the treatment given to her accepting it as her fate and also suffered nonconsensual sexual advances from her own male relatives but by the end she had seen and tolerated enough, decides to stand up for herself and for her unborn child. She declares that she shall take up on the role of the "father" for that child and take away that power from the male who is biologically the father. She gains this strength while she was carrying the baby in her belly and hence becomes qualified for being this role. She becomes adamant about her decision, does not get affected by the thought that people may not accept that baby, may also mistreat her and the child or even separate the child from her. She anyway plans to keep the child as safe as she can and give that baby a beautiful life, fulfilling the duties of a father while literally being the mother who is full of motherly affection.

> "I shall not yield. I shall bring him up myself. Whatever these people do to me, I shall create a commotion, cry, go away. But my beloved child, the fortune I have acquired after desperate trouble, I shall not throw away".

Conclusion

This paper is an attempt to point out how the writer made the narrator break off the shackles. From being a weak, powerless victim who had to face all kinds of discrimination, to becoming a stubborn rebel who makes a statement wherein, she calls herself the *father* of her child and the journey that she undergoes during this process of becoming what she became by the end is immensely overwhelming to the reader. The narrator takes up the responsibility of being the 'stronger' parent who is adamant and stubborn and has the strength to face the society and fight it to give a good life to the baby. This story shows how Chalam wished for a world which would have it's women free to revolt against all miseries that they had to go through in their lives. We see the narrator breaking off from her own negative thoughts which were a result of the society which made her doubt upon how she would raise a child who would be called father-less and would definitely one day ask her who is his father to which, she decides to answer saying, *"I am your father"* and also plans to never tell anything about the real father.

Works Cited

Indian Literature, An Introduction. "Widow." Delhi University, Anjana Neira Dev, Bajrang Bihari Tiwari, Sanam Khanna. Pearson Publications, 2006, pp. 274 – 283.

John Greene (Quote on impending fatherhood)

Web Sources

https://en.wikipedia.org/wiki/Chalam_(writer)

CHAPTER 18

The Woeful Condition of Tribal Women: Re-Contextualising Mahasweta Devi's "Draupadi" in the Present Time

Supriyo Mapder

Abstract

The Bengali writer Mahasweta Devi is well-known for her work on tribals. One of her most popular short stories is "Draupadi", where she depicts a tribal woman's resistance against societal injustices against tribals. Despite the fact that the narrative was published in 1978, its significance and context are still relevant in today's society. The plight of tribal women is examined through the lens of Mahasweta Devi's "Draupadi," underlining their primary concerns, which are still present to some extent. This paper provides a detailed analysis of the short narrative, illuminating the unique characteristics of tribal culture, their unique rites, and the reasons for their periodic uprising against the landlords. With these, this paper would question the upper-class society for being the reason behind the almost unchanged deplorable condition of the tribal society, particularly the tribal women. This paper will finish with some recent pieces of evidence that provide a reality check on the situation of indigenous women.

Keywords: Tribal Women, Tribal Community, Women Emancipation, Subaltern, Societal-Inequality.

Introduction

Tribal Community is a group of people who live in forests and hilly areas and are known for carrying out some unusual traditions and customs. According to the census 2011, tribal communities constitute 8.6% of India's population. Always classified as Untouchables, these people were introduced from the time of kings and were abused by landlords. As a result of their subjection to oppression, they rebelled from time to time. The activist and political writer, Mahasweta Devi is universally noted for always prioritising tribal life. She wrote around 100 novels and 20 collections of short stories. Among her most celebrated works, *Aranyer Adhikar (The Right Over the Forest)*, *Choti Munda evam Tar Tir* (*Choti Munda and His Arrow*), *Bashai Tudu*, *Titu Mir* all illustrate tribal life with utmost honesty. Short story collections such as "Imaginary Maps" and "Breast Stories", "Of Women, Outcastes, Peasants, and Rebels" are also no exception in their description of the marginalisation. While mourning her death in the newspaper *The Hindu*, Antara Dev Sen writes how Devi has "fiercely championed the rights of the marginalised and the disposed. And among all those she campaigned for; she was most vocal as a crusader for tribal rights" (Sen). This short story "Draupadi" is unique for associating a mere tribal woman with the mythological Draupadi (the righteous heroine of the epic *Mahabharata*) and ultimately glorifying her marginalised stature. Scholars have paid profound attention to her, acknowledging her as "a palimpsest and a contradiction" and unraveling a multitude of layers within her (Spivak 11). However, the generous treatment of Devi in demonstrating the whole community, in general, didn't get its due attention by scholars. This paper will offer a refined observation of the tribal community as represented by Devi in her short story. While examining their condition, cultures, problems, this paper will also try to relate it to the present-day scenario where the tribal's condition is still under consideration.

Mahasweta Devi's story 'Draupadi' was first published in 1978 in Bengali in her collection, *Agnigarbha*. The English translation – by Gayatri Chakravorty Spivak – came out in her collection *Breast Stories* in 1997. The backdrop to the story is the Naxalbari movement of West Bengal in which the tribal rebelled against the wealthy tyrannical landlords to break the prevailing structure. This movement first took place in a remote village in West Bengal called Naxalbari and then it started taking its gigantic shape across other regions namely Bihar, Andhra Pradesh and parts of Tamil Nadu and Uttar Pradesh (Awasthi 2). The Naxalites fight for an equal society, where everyone will have the similar economic and societal position. The tribal identity itself excludes its people from the 'mainstream society' (Dutta 42). They are considered to be the lowest in the class-based society of 20th century India (Dutta 42). Therefore, they are arguably the most degraded and oppressed. It is at this politically upheaval stage that Devi's "Draupadi" begins when "many young men and women, batch by batch and on jeeps, have attacked police station after police station, terrified and elated the region and disappeared into the forest of Jharkhani" (Devi 23).

This short story commences with two policemen, the representatives of the upper-class society, who question the naming of a tribal lady. The fact that the name Draupadi is associated with glory, being the name of the Queen of Pandavas, its use on a tribal lady diminishes its elite aura. In other words, it ruins the beauty of the name. This strikes the first Policeman and he jumps in wonder asking, "What's this, a tribal called Dopdi?" (Devi 19). These very first sentences present the upper class' view towards the tribal where their identity deprives them of having a proper name. However, her name is shortened and made into Dopdi which is probably because of the mispronouncing of the name by the uneducated classes. Further, this name is not given by Dopdi's parents but by the wife of Zaminder, Surja Sahu. Scholars have argued that this name is given as an act of benevolence. Further, Devi emphasised tribal language by making her tribal characters speak in their own language, which is completely incomprehensible for the highly educated men. Words like 'Ma-ho' and 'hendre rambra' are so unique that even tribal specialists' dictionaries failed to solve their meaning. On the one hand, it may suggest the tribal peoples' wartime skill in using special language, on the other hand, it may also hint at the fact that knowing tribal culture and language has been only a pretense since these people were probably never explored authentically.

The uncannily real description of tribal life in a remote village of West Bengal called Champabhumi is unfolded in the story. Mahasweta Devi herself was from a middle-class society but her involvement in the life of the tribal was so engaging that she draws them realistically without exaggerating or romanticising. The unique features of the tribal community as presented in the story are their union and their blind faith in each other. As Devi explains, "Crow would eat crow's flesh before Santal would betray Santal" (Devi 31). They are also known for obstinacy. They do have a strong emotional attachment with the forest and the forest is their favorite hideout. They celebrate their joy by singing a song in their language and they can ululate like police sirens:

Samaray hijulenako mar goekope
And
Hende rambra keche keche Pundi rambra keche keche (Devi 21).

For meals, they have only rice and they are unhygienic as evident in Dopdi's use of kerosene to kill lice. For medicines, they have tobacco leaves and limestone powder. They use pseudo names when they are in an operation (as Dopdi and her husband's pseudo names were Upi Majhen and Matang Majhi). They have mastered the art of guerrilla warfare and they use weapons like scythe, hatchet, and knife. It is noteworthy that if any of them are caught, they would bite their tongue off but won't let others be destroyed by them. However, the revolutionaries were betrayed by their fellow workers Shomai and Budhna, and the blame goes to their mixed breed. Furthermore, what differs the Santals from the mainstream Hindu society is the fact that their women are equal to men (Dutta 2). Dopdi doesn't stay behind bars but fights "shoulder to shoulder with her husband" (Dutta 2). She unhesitatingly took the responsibility of saving the other revolutionaries after the death of her husband. For the tribal community, Dopdi is the "peasant leader" whose relentless contribution to their society would be remembered and celebrated (Pati 6). But in the eyes of "semi-feudal social codes of Indian agricultural communities, she is a criminal and a villain" (Pati 6). This notion of equality can be questioned. Was Dopdi really an equal to the males of her society? However, if it was taken in the context of the present time, most of the tribal societies, particularly in India, are patrilineal. Today, tribal women are marginalised by the upper-class society for being tribal, secondly, by the same society for being woman, and ultimately by her own community for being a woman.

All of the tribal earn their livelihood by working in the harvests of rich landlords which refer to the oppressive feudal system. History recorded the oppressions that the minorities went through during the feudal system in the time of colonialism. One of the most important examples is the Santhal Rebellion (1855-1856) in which the tribal of Jharkhand rebelled against the tax system of the East India Company and the usury practices of Zamindars. However, even after 30 years of independence, their situation had hardly changed. They were still dependent on their livelihood and controlled by the Zamindars of their areas. One such despotic ruler was Surja Sahu who forcefully imposes a high tax on the tribal. In addition to tax, the practice of high interest for the borrowed money led the tribal's forthcoming generations to pay free labor in the harvests of Zamindars. As is the case of Dulna whose grandfather took a bit of paddy from him (Surja Sahu)" and he has to "give him free labor to repay the debt"

(Devi 30). Earning a living, particularly for indigenous women, is still a difficult task in the current scenario. Stuti Banga in her article explores the problems of tribal women after the independence of India. Concerning the livelihood of tribal women, she notes that women have a higher rate of dependence on the forest economy for their survival needs and income rendering them in a more vulnerable state in cases of degradation and deforestation in forests (Banga). This creates a dependency issue and prohibits women from becoming independent (Banga). As a result, they remain the most downtrodden members of a large patriarchal society.

Apart from this, Devi writes how during the time of drought when "everything is burning", the tribal people were refused to provide with water (Devi 30). Though digging two tube wells gave him "unlimited water", "the untouchables don't get the water" (Devi 30). This crisis with water has been presented by multiple authors. Sarat Chandra Chattopadhyay's short story "Mahesh" also presents a similar condition as Amina, being the daughter of the only Muslim family in a Hindu village of Brahmins, has always to wait for a benevolent woman to put water in her pitcher as she is forbidden to touch water (Chattopadhyay). Though the situation has largely changed, this scenario of water crisis prevailed. As Times of India reports in 2018 that according to the 2011 census, 27% of the tribal population does not have access to safe water and toilets (The Times of India). In addition to this, The Hindu reports in 2021 that the lack of roads in hilly areas prevents the way of supplying safe drinking water to the tribal (Gopal). Like, the tribal in Devi's story, the tribal communities of Ravikamatham district in Andra Pradesh, staged "a protest by keeping water containers on their heads and kneeling on the ground to draw the attention of the authorities to their woes" (Gopal).

"Sexual molestation of any form happens to be patriarchy's method of social control rather than the pathology of sexual violence as such", argues Rajeshwari Sunder Rajan in *The Story of Draupadi's Disrobing* (Rajan102). The naming of the tribal lady after the heroine of *Mahabharata* naturally evokes comparisons between them. Both of these women were an object of men's desire. But whereas *Mahabharat*'s Draupadi was publicly stripped, Dopdi was gang-raped. Dopdi is introduced as the "Most notorious female" and "Long wanted by many" (Devi 20). Her femininity attracts the lust of upper-class policemen who, considering her as weak, has madly hunted her, "Catch Dopdi, she will lead us to others". However, this is not the first time that Dopdi is turned into an object of sexual desire. Surja Sahu, who on the one hand, has spitted on them, calling out her inferior untouchable identity; on the other, his "mouth watered when he looked at" Dopdi (Devi30). Similarly, Mulk Raj Anand's *Untouchable* also enlightens such hypocritical attitude of an Upper-class Brahmin, who was about to molest an untouchable girl, Sohini, the sister of the protagonist Bakha (Anand 24). These recurring episodes evidence the fact that a tribal woman was always a sexual object for the upper class. One of the most brutal practices was the "breast tax" system which was imposed on tribal women in some particular places in 19th century India. In the 19th century, some places in India practiced a "Breast tax system" in which tribal women (particularly people from Ezhava and Nadar) were forced to pay taxes for their breasts. The upper-caste men were the ones who collected this tax. "The larger the breasts, the higher the tax", writes Adeleke (Adeleke).

Apart from this, the rape of tribal women during war is also highlighted in the story. During a war, American soldiers camped in Shiandanga and they used tribal women as sexual devices. As a result of the sexual union with the tribal women, the tribal society has now flooded with half-breed Santhals. Dopdi takes pride in her forefathers because they protected their ladies from American soldiers. Even at present, the sexual abuse of tribal women is one of the most debated issues. However, these issues are overlooked and didn't get much attention from the media. In 2016, eight tribal women from Chattisgarh accused the security forces of repeatedly gang-raping and physically torturing them. Published in *The Hindu,* the report says that many tribal women from the village have been gang-raped by the security forces and out of them only 12 women came to the police. Further, it was also informed by the local sources that the police were initially unwilling to register the complaint (*The Hindu*). Prof Debartai Halder and Jaishankar Karuppannan pointed out in their essay how in the Andaman Islands tribal women have been used as sexual objects by tourists. These women were half-naked and were forced to dance before the tourists (Halder and Karuppannan). The use of tribal women as sex gadgets has worsened their situation. Currently, the increased spread of Sexually Transmitted Diseases (STDs), mostly HIV/AIDS, is another challenge that indigenous women face (Banga). The tribes of Nagaland express grave worry about AIDS spread among tribal women (Banga). The levels have risen to the point that the neighboring state of Manipur is also in jeopardy (Banga). These reports thus voice against all the injustices inflicted on tribal people and implore for their safeguarding, which is still not happening. All the tribal Dopdis are still in need of protection from the Govt.

The most remarkable aspect of the story is its ending which explosively subverts the dynamics of power. Senanayak, the representative of the elite, educated society, initially appears as a very professional man; and as the story unfolds its preceding layers, his hypocrisy is properly perceived by the readers. However, his apparent image of an intelligent man with a specialisation in Combat, who claims that "to capture the enemy, become one", is completely changed into the main villain of the story (Devi 22). His initial identification with the tribal community may lead him to his success at capturing Dopdi but the lurking hypocrisy in him and his belongingness to the Upper-Class society fail him at comprehending the true nature of a tribal lady. When the tribal woman Dopdi was apprehended near the end of the story, she was taken to the camp and a questioning episode took place. Senanayak's failure to extract information from her made him angry. He instructed other policemen to "make her" and "do the needful", implying to ravish her repeatedly as long as their aim is not achieved (Devi 34). Throughout the night the tribal woman was brutally violated. As Devi pitifully questions, "How many came to make her?... How many? Four-five-six-seven" (Devi 35).

An educated administrative man like Senanayak was meant to protect the tribal woman. He was supposed to be her savior. But his refusal to be so and his emphasis on doing the 'needful' actually represents the authoritative figures' hypocritical attitude towards the tribal which ultimately deteriorated their position. This treatment of a tribal lady and the upper class' indifferent attitude towards this doleful incident inevitably enlighten the awareness of the modern readers, who not only realise the actual condition of the tribal communities but also their participation in perpetuating their hopeless condition. As Dr. Haseena V.A in her essay comments that "violence against tribal women is not a new or recent phenomenon. Women had been the victims of violence all through the ages – in all societies, culture, religion; and religious communities of the world" (V.A).

Devi however subverts this victimisation and turned it into a celebration of protest. Though Spivak in her Foreword to the short story writes, "As a tribal, Dopdi is not romanticised by Mahasweta", this statement is debatable (Spivak 11). One woman, who has been gang-raped throughout the night and whose "thigh and pubic hair matted with dry blood" and "two breasts, two wounds", can stand and confront Senanayak. This final scene makes Dopdi Mejhen, a superwoman. Her refusal to dress up herself can be viewed as her rejection to be "the second sex" as referred to by Simone de Beauvoir. Dopdi aspires to be the "Super Sex". She confronts the Upper-Class representative and displays her mutilated body, which has been caused solely by their careless and non-involving attitude toward the tribal classes. Excluding their nonparticipation, the damage that they cause aggravated their distress. Thus, this short story here becomes a motivational space where an example like Dopdi helps the tribal women to protest against injustice and to confront their enemies with vigor and bravery.

Conclusion

The condition of tribal has slowly been changing but the tribal men and women still do face so many disapprovals, which ultimately reduces their growth. Even today there are many villages in India where the tribal communities are still considered to be untouchables. They are not allowed to enter the temples. In 2016, Chitralekha, a Dalit woman, spoke out against the authoritative classes. She declares how her decision to earn her livelihood by driving autorickshaws was disapproved by the males of the upper caste and how her family was attacked repeatedly for it. The males of the upper caste have even destroyed her autorickshaw. She added, "they couldn't afford to have me in their space, since I am a Dalit Woman" (Chitralekha). This short story "Draupadi" can also be conceived as a microcosmic presentation of the macrocosmic degradation faced by the tribal women. Like Devi's Dopdi who refuses to be the victim and confronts the educated man for her rights, here Chitralekha also refuses to stop and continues her fight against the educated upper class of the society. Like Dopdi, Chitralekha is also "a subaltern who can speak" (Spivak).

Thus, in this short pan, Devi justifiably illustrates the tribal society along with its unique cultural, and social characteristics, which are not too unfamiliar to the tribal communities of today's society.

People of Upper-class used the history of the tribal as a means of remembrance without really recognising their struggles and hardships. But Devi, through her relentless involvement with the tribal classes, wrote their history in a translucent manner, subverting their marginalised stature. As she, being the mother of the sabar, writes in *Imaginary Maps*, "They want to feel proud that they are tribal" (Devi). It can be argued that the superiority of the upper class and their refusal to accept the tribal as equal has been one of the foremost reasons that deteriorate their situation. It is only through the acceptance of their culture and lifestyle that they can reach great heights.

Works Cited

Anand, Mulk Raj. *Untouchable.* Penguin Books, 1940.

Awasthi, Sonali and Ayush Mishra. "The Naxalite Movement in India," *IJLMH,* vol.1, no.4, 2018. IJLMH, www.ijlmh.com, Accessed 4 January2022.

Banga, Stuti. "Gender Issues Faced by Tribal Women in Post-Independence India", *Sociology Group,* Gender Issues Faced by Tribal Women in Post-Independence India (sociologygroup.com).

Dahat, Pavan. "Eight Tribal Women Allege Gang-Rape by Security Forces in Bijapur". *The Hindu,* https://www.thehindu.com/news/national/other-states/Eight-tribal-women-allege-gang-rape-by-security-forces-in-Bijapur/article14014055.ece. Accessed 23 Dec 2021.

Devi, Mahasweta. "Draupadi". *Breast Stories.* Translated By Gayetri Chakroborty Spivak. *Seagull Books,*1978.

Devi, Mahasweta. *Imaginary Maps: Three Stories by Mahasweta Devi.* Translated By Gayetri Chakroborty Spivak. Routledge, https://doi.org/10.4324/9780203760116.

Dutta, Bhaskar Chandra. "Questioning Subalternity: Re-reading Mahasweta Devi's 'Draupadi'", *Journal of Research in Humanities and Social Science*, vol.7, no. 2. 2019, pp.41-43. *Quest Journal*, www.questjournals.org. Accessed 28 December 2021.

Gopal, B. Madhu. "Safe Drinking water eludes tribal people in Agency", *The Hindu.* 14 March 2021. https://www.thehindu.com/news/national/andhra-pradesh/safe-drinking-water-eludes-tribal-people-in-agency/article34068772.ece.

Halder, Debarati and Jaishankar Karuppannan. "Online Victimisation of Andaman Jarawa Tribe Women: An Analysis of the 'Human Safari' Youtube Videos (012) and Its Effects". *British Journal Of Criminology*, May 2014. doi:10.1093/bjc/azu026.

Pati, Mitali. R. Mahasweta Devi's Rhetoric of Subversion in "Draupadi", *South Asian Review*, 2017, pp. 86-91, https://doi.org/10.1080/ 02759527.1996.11932202, Accessed 26 December, 2021.

Rajan, Rajeshwari Sundar, editor. The Story of Draupadi's Disrobing:Meanings for our Times". *Gender Issues in Post-Independence India*, Kali Publishers, 1991.

Sen, Dev Antara." Indefatigable Chronicler of the Oppressed". *The Hindu*, https://www.thehindu.com/books/Indefatigable-chronicler-of-the-oppressed/article14513287.ecew.th. Accessed 23 dec,2021.

Spivak, Gayetri Chakroborty. *Can the Subaltern Speak?: Reflections on The History of An Idea.* Columbia University Press, 2010.

V.A, Dr.Haseena. "Tribal Women as the Victims of the Interrelation between the Empowerment and Domestic Violence in Kerala", *Paripex – Indian Journal of Research,* Vol.4, no.2, 2015.

"9 Problems Faced by Indian Tribals – Explained". *Your Article Library*, https://www.yourarticlelibrary.com/society/indian-society/9-main-problems-faced-by-indian-tribals-explained/39243. Accessed 23Dec, 2021.

CHAPTER 19

Queering the Woman-Widow: Visiting this Gender as an Oxymoron!

Ms. Suparna Roy

Abstract

The cultural organisation and match-making sensation of traditional patterns has often resulted in numerous power discourses to mould bodies in definitive patterns of acceptance/rejection. Judith Butler's careful explanation of what a women can be has really deconstructed the monolith identity patriarchy created for them, and which Queer lens has allowed us to perceive enthusiastically; also Nivedita Menon in her work *Seeing Like A Feminist* (2012) stated – "Feminism is thus not about individual men and women, but about understanding the ways in which 'men' and 'women' are produced and inserted into patriarchies that differ according to time and place" (Menon, 7). The cultural construction of women as a stabilised solid and presumable umbrella veils the intersectional experience of woman. While moving from the mainstream marginalised narratives, when our focus shifts to the peripheral markers of this intricately designed society, we could possibly engage into the tales of identities whose stories are far from the centred discursive domain. The concept of multiculturalism has resurged paths to analyse literature and its conscious flow of psychic emotions in a beautiful pattern; wherein, social complexities and voice of repulsion regarding all forms of violence is echoingly strong. From this domain of theorising experiences into clear shells of printed words, strong enough to portray the realistic political apartheid followed under cultural excuses is highly valuable. Therefore, this short article attempts to present the renderings of the widows and widowhood, and how they simultaneously function as an oxymoron within the phallogocentric cultural practices.

Keywords: women, gender, widows, widower, culture

Introduction

The term 'queer' has made a protracted adventure; in phrases of the definitions it meant and has touched on meanings that are greatly exclusive but rather linked. The preliminary means of the phrase dates lower back to 1508 Scotland, in which it meant strange, peculiar. Close to 1812, the phrase advanced to mean 'to spoil, ruin' and become used as a verb. Only after a hundred years, in 1935, it began getting used as a noun withinside the area of homosexual. However the term queer is open-ended and it is indeed important to know how this open-endedness of the term 'queer' has made itself politically more efficacious. Queer activists Gayle Rubin's article argues that ideas about sexuality are structured strategically in binary oppositions, where one side is positive, good, moral, strong, and right and the other side is negative, bad, immoral, weak and wrong. Sexuality has thus then become nothing more than a commodity. As described by Judith Butler –

> My understanding of queer is a term that desires that you don't have to present an identity card before entering a meeting. Heterosexuals can join the queer movement. Bisexuals can join the queer movement. Queer is not being lesbian. Queer is not being gay. Queer is an argument against certain normativity, what a proper lesbian or gay identity is.

Thus, Queer/queering means to protest against any normative structure; Queer becomes a term which embraces more fluid categories, does not binarise, and most importantly provides humans with a peculiar lens to view any normativity of socio-cultural threads. The diversity and fluidity of queer has made it accessible to and applicable in the intricately designed world of literary theories! Therefore Queer will always remain politically radical, the radicalism which first perpetuated the movement against normativity. The ambiguity of the word queer has indeed benefitted political activism and has functioned as an emancipatory notion because it has no fixed referent. So, 'queer theory' is broadly used to resist patriarchal dichotomies, heteronormativity and to pull out the oppressive subjugation of all bodies particularly women and other minorities by disclosing the underlying power structures that produce.

Theoretical Interpretations

Why Queering is important here? Judith Butler enchantingly stated Queer means an argument against any normativity, so the 'normative' definition of women must be queered to bring out the sufferings of the widows, by critiquing the underlying power-structures that produces the widow and widower. Women and the concept of 'what a woman is' has repeatedly revisited the definable spaces of socio-literary and political domain in phases and faces that are re-presented within the patriarchally coveted Brahminical hierarchies. The definition and conceptualisation of the objective women has been enlisted by personalities according to the political interpretation of the body identified as women, and what it is, when placed amidst the complexities of phallus-power discourse. To remember Simone de Beauvoir regarded women are 'marked in absence' so rules are imposed on them, but men are considered 'universal' hence they are invisibly present like omnipotent fundamental organisms. Therefore, the construction of a woman's identity is circulated and trapped within the 'beating and molesting' survival, where patience and tolerance measures the skin's ability to accept and move on. Within the Indian spectrum, the viable ideal formation of 'women' is when they associated and adhere to the forever 'sacrificial framework' of the 'self', which is in a way easier for the women and unquestionable too, for they do not know what to question. Judith Butler's careful explanation of what a women can be has really deconstructed the monolith identity patriarchy created for them, and which Queer lens has allowed us to perceive enthusiastically; Butler stated – "Women are the sex which is not 'one'. Within a phallogocentric language, women constitute the *unrepresentable*…women represent the sex that cannot be thought, a linguistic absence and opacity". The cultural construction of women as a stabilised solid and presumable umbrella veils the intersectional experience of woman. Hence it is crucial to critique identity-solidifying discourses with variability of experiences. Who is a widow? Adhering to the binarised structures that refuse to accept the hues, definition of a widow is associated with the body of a woman, for widow is a noun here but more appropriately receives the 'object' position within the syntactical framework. Power discourse constructed widow as the woman who will be widowed by the death of the partner; means the one who will be on the receiving end of the widowhood, not the maker of the widow. Thus, the widow then by linguistic position becomes a powerless word of identity; a word that is pitied and victimised. Now, a widower is also a noun but that receives a subject-position in the syntactical relation, for widower is the person in power of widowing a body, an identity. So, widows are 'created' by widowers, which means power-discourse framed a masculine noun-widower to indicate the power of a phallus even after their death, to control, the identity of a woman, so using the power pattern thereby the feminine noun indicates-widow. Here these words – widow and widower are clearly adhering to the computing binary of identities. Putting the queer lens to it, I find that the definitive features associated with these terms are problematic. A widow has to be woman wearing white, naming God, without any symbols of color and desires, and I ask why. Red is a color linked with the symbol of marriage in India, but since childhood every woman wears red, then why suddenly only as a marker is red associated? Secondly, red is also indicative of vibrant life, desire, but I question why a 20 year old widow cannot be vibrant and have desire, but can be sold to prostitution to get desire out of her body; what is wrong with that or even why a 80 year old widow cannot have so? These questions pricks those solidifying monolithically dominating patriarchal powers who constructed identities as fixed and its features must never be questioned, a reason for which the widows of Varanasi suffers.

The presentation of women oscillates as per operating domains. In India the concept of women draws an intricate intersectional perception, for it keeps altering like the diversity we have. The concept of women strongly channelises the idea of widows; a fear is installed in them as to 'what would happen to them without their husband', for women and their definitions as Irigaray regarded was defined by men and established in relation to the phallus. The fear of 'what will happen to me' was less than the fear of what society would do to me. The minds of women were so beautifully ingrained with dark ritualistic hues that they feared the life in the 'absence' of her husband. An important issue to regard here is the *absence-presence*. Until the presence of the husband the women is the wife (a linguistic absence and a marked presence), but the moment this husband figure dies, the wife is the widow who suddenly becomes the absently marked presence; a fright starts evolving within her psychic framework now what; hence all regulations on the body. We must understand that rules are not imposed on the identity-widow; rather, on the body-women who is a widow! The issue of widows burning or killing themselves can be seen even in Independent India, few such cases includes-

- April15, in Maharashtra a woman's body was found in her husband's pyre, where her age was recognised to be 50years old
- December, 2014, a 65 year old woman jumps into her husband's funeral pyre in Bihar, Saharsa district

- 14th October, 2008 – relatives were arrested when police came to know they 'watched' the 75 year old woman burning herself along with her husband's pyre
- 22nd September, 2006 – Brothers were arrested for throwing their 95 year old mother into the funeral of her husband

Cultural dimensions operating with India has framed excuses to keep going the patriarchal approaches to widowhood. The issue of Varanasi can be also traced with Religious cultural power-play. Varanasi is a centre of Hindu worshippers and priests, that means, majorly Brahmins are the rulers of the place. The notion of controlling and regulating bodies and identities churned from the time Brahmins replace and reformed the Vedic system and believes; position of women started degrading since then, as 'history' marks. Varanasi therefore is already a land of pure religion without liberty of religious choices; thereby a place of subjugation clearly. Now the different subject-position of women in such a pure religious phallogocentric society is doubly oppressed. So, what happens to widows there? Commencing from colors to hair styles all gets curbed through and under the lens of patriarchal rules, for women and widows of Varanasi are not defined as they wish to define themselves; instead are defined as patriarchal gazes and believes wishes to re-present their lives-identities-stories under the veil and excuse of religious-purity. Now this culture has produced widows as an 'outcasts' to our social organisation. Women's presentation has always been in association with men – they are the daughters/ the wives/the mothers; roles that are organised intricately in connection to the 'unshifting' position of men – the subjects! In Varanasi the widows are pariahs; some are old as eighty years while some are young as twenty years. The older ones begs with their rotten skin and empty stomach to earn for their food; while he younger ones are thrown into prostitution to suffer until their skin are rotten and they start begging! Further oppression of widows includes –

- Widows are made to lose their lofty shiny hairs, colors of life, and sexual desire after the death of their husbands; they are to give their lives in the service of God or violence, or serve as sex-slaves for all phallus customers. They are not even provided with the chance to explore as to whether or not they desire or hate a phallus.
- The oppression and horrendous condition woman has nothing to do with "natural" rules (rules are never natural),

rather it is very much a cultural product turned into destined futures for the gender – women. *After the death of their husband remaining untouched is the way to go to heaven or burning the flesh along with the funeral pyre of the husband is the way to reach heaven.* In association to this quoting a misogynistic line from the texts of Agni Purana which states that – "…The widow who practices self-control and austerities after the death of her husband, goes to heaven…the widow who burns herself on the same funeral pyre with her husband also goes to heaven" (222.19-23).

- Sadly, therefore practices of getting bald, getting white(s) on heads and body, forgetting the individual existence of the self, results in a horrific future for these women. The home which recognised them as a part of it turns hostile and just throws them out; a huge sense of uncanny reverberates through all known relationships under the name of culture.
- Abandoned by society these widows often seek shelter in ashrams, where their fat have no assurance.
- Coming to Varanasi as widows to hope for 'a home in the heaven' after their death to find peace and reclamation as Varanasi is associated with Lord Shiva, alternatively kills their left years of lives too.
- Census figures states how Uttar Pradesh has the largest population of children marrying; more than 2.9 million of children between 18-19 years old are married off to old men, resulting in younger widows.

Conclusion

The situation of a woman's identity as the 'oxymoron' presentation now needs a stoppage, where every time woman must not be visualised within the structural binary if pure/impure, wife/whore and angel/devil and so on. The *religious veil* of Varanasi instigates and fuels the exploitation of widows there, a voice that needs to be heard! Since people are hardly aware of the knowledge provided within Gita and Vedic and Upanishada readings; particularly women are hardly allowed to enter the reading of these texts; often the phallus power moulds it as per their need. The 20 year old getting widowed is given to prostitution by a priest, no one questions. The widow is said to live with the priest for cleansing her soul of all 'dirt/pollution' and then the priests rapes her body and after dong out with his lust dumps her into prostitution. Religious pyres frame widowhood and its rules. Since within a phallogocentric society everything is phallus-oriented, the resulted rules of widowhood are also to cramp women. These incidents start with child marriage. Majority of them suffers from HIV positive health impacts. The duplicable removal of widows from society as 'outcasts' has resulted in more than 38000 in number, where 12000+ women are between the age of 20-45. Varanasi is known not only as the land of widows but also a religious land; hence, religious blindness, lack of educational awareness results in the phallus-dominated religion to rule the bodies. The exclusion of widows and seclusion of their identities are therefore results of extreme patriarchal religious acts. Thus the objectification and suppression of women from and under diversifies layers is still a question that is composed under silent discourse. Within this cultural heterogeneity of India this subjugative power regime that commodifies women from birth to death and turns their lives to a living hell needs discussion, urgently. It is very important now that we stop pitying the widows as victims of our religion(s), and start discussing and questioning the religious features which makes and constructs these objective widows.

Works Cited

Butler, Judith. *Gender Trouble.* Routledge, 1990.

"Brothers Arrested for Throwing 95-Year-Old Mother on Funeral Pyre." *Daily Mail Online*, Associated Newspapers, 22 Sept. 2006, https://www.dailymail.co.uk/news/article-406471/Brothers-arrested-throwing-95-year-old-mother-funeral-pyre.html.

DNA WEB Team. "Maharashtra: Woman's Body Found from Husband's Pyre." *DNA India*, 2015, https://www.dnaindia.com/india/report-maharashtra-woman-s-body-found-from-husband-s-pyre-2073728.

Menon, Nivedita. *Seeing Like A Feminist.* UK: Penguin, 2012.

Niswade, Jyoti. "Social Neglect and Oppression of Widows in Rural India: Need for Social, Economic and Policy Implications." *Research in Political Sociology*, 2015, pp. 113–131., https://doi.org/10.1108/s0895-993520150000023008.

Shrivastava, Nidhi. "The Progress of Indian Women from 1900s to Present." *Honors Scholar Theses*, 10 May 2009, opencommons.uconn.edu /srhonors_theses/76/?utm_source=opencommons.uconn.edu%2Fsrhonors_theses%2F76&utm_medium=PDF&utm_campaign=PDFCoverPages. Accessed 18 June 2022.

"In Bihar, 65-Year-Old Woman Jumps into Husband's Funeral Pyre-India News, Firstpost." *Firstpost*, 15 Dec. 2014, https://www.firstpost.com/india/bihar-65-year-old-woman-jumps-husbands-funeral-pyre-1849693.html.

"Relatives Arrested after Widow Burns to Death on Funeral Pyre." *The Guardian*, Guardian News and Media, 14 Oct. 2008, https://www.theguardian.com/world/2008/oct/14/india.

"Relatives Arrested after Widow Burns to Death on Funeral Pyre." *The Guardian*, Guardian News and Media, 14 Oct. 2008, https://www.theguardian.com/world/2008/oct/14/india.

Vlassoff, Carol. "The Situation of Widows: Do Sons and Brothers Help?" *Gender Equality and Inequality in Rural India*, 2013, pp. 137–156., https://doi.org/10.1057/9781137373922_8.

CHAPTER 20

Portrayal of Women in the Cinema *The Great Indian Kitchen*: A Comparative Study

Nahan N. K

Abstract

Our society has been enslaved by male patriarchy for generations. It can be found in every aspect of our lives. Movies that purport to depict real-life situations are no exception. Our cinema has primarily depicted male dominance in its narration over the years. Female characters are frequently reduced to supporting roles and used as a marketable commodity. The film industry has consistently failed to depict women's real-life problems. Women were once considered second-class citizens in the film industry. The film 'The Great Indian Kitchen' becomes relevant in this context.

Mr. Joe Baby, the film's scriptwriter and director, stands out from the crowd. He tries to become the voice of the oppressed women who have been confined within the four walls of their homes. He attempts to depart from the traditional method, and the language he employs provides the audience with a fresh perspective.

How Women are Treated in Society

For generations, Indian society has been ruled by patriarchy, in which males wield primary power and rule both society and family. Males do not value women and regard them as an object to which they must perform all housework and satisfy their sexual desires. This is evident in every aspect of our society. As a cinema, it is to depict real life in society, but up until a few years ago, women were only used as a second heroine or for item songs. All of this suggests that not only in society, but also in the film industry, women are given minor roles and are portrayed as second-class citizens.

Male dominance can be seen not only in front of, but also behind, the film industry. There will be more male directors or producers in film because women do not receive the same opportunities and support as men do from society. Even if a male director returns to the cinema after his first film is a flop, every audience will give him a second chance, but for women, getting the same chance and encouragement from the people is a pipe dream; even coworkers will make them mock in front of everyone. Not only does society regard them as a second class citizen or an object devoid of feelings or emotions.

However, the cinema has evolved significantly in recent years, with more emphasis placed on female roles. Many films are now directed by women; even male directors direct their films and give significant roles to women rather than men. There is a lot of cinema that is written specifically for women. Previously, the film industry failed to consistently depict women's real-life problems, but now cinema has begun to portray women's real-life experiences in society and the stress that they face. There are numerous films in which only female actors perform. All of this demonstrates how far film has progressed.

The director tells the story of an oppressed married woman in Indian society in 'The Great Indian Kitchen.' The writer takes on the role of the struggling women trapped within the four walls of the house.

The writer attempts to depart from traditional methods, and the language he employs provides the audience with a fresh perspective. These types of films are extremely rare in the Malayalam film industry.

The Great Indian Kitchen' is the most powerful patriarchal film. The film depicts a newly married couple and demonstrates how a woman struggles to be a submissive wife to her husband. The most striking aspect of this film is that not all men are angry or violent toward their wives; there are some men who speak softly and impose their will on the women like a slow poison, as depicted in this film. Suraj Venjaramoodu plays the husband, and Nimisha Sajayan plays the wife.

At first, everyone thinks he is a perfect husband for Nimisha, who loves and cares for her, but after a few days, it becomes clear that he sees her only as an object for fulfilling his sexual desires and preparing and serving food for him. Even his father is unconcerned about her. The father in law advises her not to work at a dance school and emphasises that a woman's responsibility is to care for her husband and family. The main point is that the characters in this film do not have names, implying that the story is about many families in which women struggle greatly under patriarchal society.

In one instance, Nimisha inquires of Suraj whether there is any difference in table manners inside and outside the home. However, in the following scene, she is lovingly forced to apologise to him and reluctantly participates in sexual acts with him. This film depicts not only patriarchal society, but also impurities associated with menstruation in Hindu religion. Everyone gives her a separate room during her periods and asks her to take a bath in a nearby river. This scene conveys the impression that Nimisha has considered no one in her husband's home during this situation. She is not permitted to prepare food for her husband at this time because Suraj is visiting Sabarimala.

This film fully discusses patriarchy, but it also discusses oppressed women who never question their husbands. Finally, Nimisha bursts out and flees the house, indicating that she is now free of all restrictions imposed by Suraj. However, the film concludes with him remarrying the other women, and the same situation occurs.

How Films Depict Women in Older Days

Film is a moving image that plays an important role in everyone's life. In reality, a film depicts the day-to-day life of every human being. However, the majority of the film industry has failed in this process because most films feature women as minor characters and men as major characters. Females were frequently depicted as second-class citizens in old films.

For many decades, significant roles were only played by men, and women were treated as a sexual object. Through each female role, the directors demonstrate a negative attitude toward society, implying that women are only for fulfilling male sexual needs and caring for the home and children. In recent years, men have played important roles in all films, while women have been portrayed as characters who must obey what others say. Here are a few examples of movies:

Veruthe oru bharya (A Wife for Nothing)

This film demonstrates that every woman must silently bear everything in her life by performing all housekeeping chores. Actually, this film demonstrates that all females have their own identities and play an important role in the family, just like the other members. Women work unpaid in their own homes. The message conveyed by this film is that women deserve to be respected for their efforts in caring for their children and performing household chores. As a result, all females must develop self-esteem. So, in this film, Akku Akbar portrays women as playing an important role in the family.

Rathinirvedham (Venereal Disenchantment)

In this film, a woman is viewed as a sexual object to satisfy all men in life. The entire costume was portrayed in a vulgar manner. Because of her body, all of the characters have a sexual attraction to her. In this film, women are treated as objects that must fulfil the needs of men in society.

Because India is a patriarchal society, all males in the society regard women as merely mother, sister, and wife who must sacrifice all dreams for their loved ones, so in the past, all Malayalam films portrayed women characters as they desired. In the movies, she was never given a significant role. Previous films clearly demonstrated that females are silent creatures who never speak up about anything. They are a symbol of endurance. Even if their husbands do something wrong, they must tolerate it for the sake of their family.

Innathe chinthavishayam (Thought for the Day)

This film depicts the lives of three women who are estranged from their husbands. Their partners all have different issues. However, this film demonstrates that even if the male character does something wrong, the female character must tolerate it and never oppose it. As the three females leave their home and live alone, another male actor, Gopakumar, enters their lives and attempts to reunite them.

Through this film, everyone learns that women are figures who sacrifice all of their needs and are not allowed to live alone in the world. That is, women are nothing without men.

Makeup Man

This film portrays the female lead actress as a negative character. When she gets a chance to act in a film, her husband becomes her makeup artist to take care of her. However, this film portrays an anger towards the female character because she is portrayed as a woman who abandons her husband and lives her own life. So society gains sympathy for men and anger for women as a result of this film, but she only acts in films because it is her husband's wish, and even when he tells her not to, she ignores him.

The exact reason for it was the women's desire to obtain funds to pay off all of her husband's debts. But the male character never understands such feelings and uses her as a symbol of selfishness. As a result, this film portrays women in a negative light at the time.

The Malayalam film industry has evolved significantly, and there are now many female-oriented films as well as female directors. Women are no longer primarily considered in films as they were in the past, and films without male actors can be seen. Or women are given more important roles than men.

Comparative Study

This is a new theme in Malayalam film industry and portraying the real life of married women who struggle hardly. Before this type of movies arrive the director give importance to male actors and their actions in film but now this all have been changed a lot and started to focus more on the story line of the cinema. The directors the producers only will cast the person who is suit for this script more than selecting big actors.

This film, "The Great Indian Kitchen," differs from other films in many ways, including the lack of a name for any of the characters who appear in it. This film does not tell the story of a family, but rather of all Indian women who face problems after their marriage. Today, many women face similar forms of oppression and lack the courage to speak out about it.

Husband works as a teacher and teaches about family values and how to build a strong foundation for a family, but in his personal life, he treats his wife as a second class citizen and does not value her. Every scene in this movie says a thousand words. The director depicts two types of women in this film: one who believes that scarifying life for husband and children is a good job, and the other who wants to work but her father-in-law says that household jobs are more beautiful than any other. Even when she got a job, no one let her go to work.

Another distinction in this film is that many scenes are taken from the kitchen. Everyone can notify from the movie that Nimisha spends most of her time in the kitchen doing housework. Many scenes are shown repeatedly, but no one gets bored because it happens in everyone's house. There is no background music in this cinema, other than the sound of washing dishes and preparing food. Everyone can find parallels in this film to their own lives.

In other films, there is little religious struggle faced by women, but in this film, it can be seen that while she is in her menstruation period, everyone thinks she is impure and lacks the purity to do any work, and she is treated as a stranger at home. Her husband did not even approach her while on his way to Sabarimala because she is impure.

There are no songs or dances in this movie that you can see in other movies. However, this film begins with a dance class and ends with the same dance class in which she became free of all restrictions imposed by her husband. Joe Baby, the director, depicts the true figure of Indian patriarchal society in this film. In real life, there are no songs, dances, or entertainments like those seen in movies.

Some shots in this film are unique to the Malayalam film industry, such as a wife leaving her husband's shoes because he is leaving the house, and another man getting up by eating food and leaving a mess for his wife to clean. This can be deduced from the film 'The Great Indian Kitchen,' in which her mother-in-law provides shoes when her father leaves, as well as small items such as paste and brushes. However, in one scene, it can be seen that while the mother went to her daughter's home, the father in law waited for Nimisha to bring him everything. These are not made up scenes; they are from people's homes. A man's wife should be like a Devi, giving lots of love and sacrificing their life for the happiness of others. Even the art director and the customer were successful in giving the actors and their home a traditional look.

There isn't much dialogue or preaching in this film, but the story is powerful and honest. Even in this film, the recurring shot of women cleaning, cooking food and sweeping depicts the female's never-ending cycle.

Suraj and Nimisha played a loving couple in another film, 'Thondimuthalum Driksakshiyum' (The Mainour and the Witness), but in this film, 'The Great Indian Kitchen,' they were an arranged marriage couple who never understood his wife's feelings.

There are numerous moments in the film that demonstrate Joe Baby's brilliance as a director. The mother-in-law wearing salwar suits when she visits her daughter's home, away from her husband's gaze, the request for two types of tea and the calling of a plumber for repairs, which never occurred. The photographs on the walls also show that women struggled greatly after marriage, regardless of generation.

All of these differences indicate that 'The Great Indian Kitchen' is distinct from other films that place a premium on women and their actions. Joe Baby doesn't have many big actors in this film; he cast only actors he thought were suitable. This film is based on your, my, and everyone else's real lives. That is why, after watching this film, everyone feels a sense of despondency.

Conclusion

In every section of Indian society, women are treated as oppressed citizens who face numerous challenges from married life and even their own religion. All men believed that women were second-class citizens with no right to question their husbands. This type of female character is even depicted in films.

The film 'The Great Indian Kitchen' is a well-known example of women's life because it depicts the real struggle faced by married women who are unable to question their husbands due to their unlimited love for them. In our society, women lacks the courage to stand out and act boldly like men; they are regarded as second-class citizens, with everyone suppressing their feelings for the selfishness of others.

Even in other films, women are not treated equally with men. They were only cast as supporting actors and were never given significant roles in the industry. This type of thing can be found in every section of Indian society.

The most touching scene in the film 'The Great Indian Kitchen' is when the wall is surrounded by pictures of married couples from different generations, and the background music plays as the sound of housekeeping chores. All of this indicates that every woman in that generation faced the same difficulties. Because there is no background music other than the sound from the kitchen, this film feels very realistic.

No one calls their name in this film, implying that it is the story of every family dealing with the same issue. This is a simple film with no big actors, and the costumes and surroundings are all traditional, giving the impression that 'The Great Indian Kitchen' is a realistic film about ordinary people. This film depicts not only the lives of women after marriage, but also the Hindu religious aspects of menstruation. All men in their caste considered those times to be impure and seeing women as a stranger at the time. Also, disregard their feelings or the fact that even husbands are not ready to see their wives at that time. These kinds of things can be seen even now.

By depicting such scenes in the film 'The Great Indian Kitchen,' director Joe Baby ushers in a new era for the Malayalam film industry. These types of films, which depict the real-life struggles of every female figure, are uncommon to see. For every man, a woman is a Devi who gives everything for her husband but no one in their family cares about them; for everyone, she is a person who does all housework and adjusts their life. This film is honest to all segments of Indian society.

Work Cited

Pillai, Anjali R. "Thappad and the Great Indian Kitchen: Is the Conversation around Female Emancipation and Women's Agency Changing in India Films?" *SheThePeople TV*, SheThePeople, 11 Mar. 2021, www.shethepeople.tv/top-stories/opinion/thappad-and-the-great-indian-kitchen/.

Pudippedi, Haricharan. "The Great Indian Kitchen Review: Powerful Film on Patriarchy and Men-Governed Traditions." *Hindustan Times*, 16 Jan. 2021, www.hindustantimes.com/entertainment/the-great-indian-kitchen-review-powerful-film-on-patriarchy-101610792874537.html.

Thomas, Rosemol. "Evolution of Female Characters in Malayalam Cinema from 1990s till Now." *Education Today*, 22 Apr. 2022, educationtoday.org.in/2022/04/22/evolution-of-female-characters-in-malayalam-cinema-from-1990s-till-now/.

CHAPTER 21

Identity of Women in Society

Deepa Sharma

Abstract

Gender identity is described as a singular start of oneself as male or female. This thought is actually connected with the idea of orientation job, which is described as the superficial presentations of character that reflect orientation character. In the advanced time, women in India were given opportunities and rights, i.e. the opportunity of articulation and fairness as well as the right to be taught. Women are the fundamental regulators of children and older people in every country of the world. Worldwide assessments show that when the economy and political relationship of an overall population change, ladies begin to stand out in helping the family with changing as per new genuine variables and challenges. The present studies focus on how all the more likely to plan women to address these difficulties by concentrating on their literature. The researcher's schooling, and work, with regard to distinctions in sexual orientation, faced by women and investigate logical inconsistencies and systemic issues that appear to impact the lead and understanding of follow-up examinations. Gender inequality affects women working capacity, job satisfaction, mental position, the efficiency of work, *etc.* Beginning time immemorial, a daughter was taking a burden on her parents. That's why parents do the early marriage of their daughters. The condition of women in India has changed over various times. Their position was very petty in our history. All practices are against the women i.e. dowry system, sati-pratha, child marriage, widow remarriage, female infanticide, *etc.* During the British Rule, several freedom fighters fully dedicated their hard work to the advancement of women. Martha Mault née Mead was accurately linked through spearheading the education in addition to preparing girls inside south India. This schooling was on earliest meet through close by a barrier, as it contradicted belief.

Keywords: Women, Norms, Beliefs, Gender Discrimination, Society, Stereotyping.

Introduction

At this point, after independence from British rule, women needed to battle with their current issues in their families. since our general public is completely male-ruled. Women are considered genuine nitwits, and they couldn't make better and more viable choices for their families. Then again, men reserves the privilege to do anything they wish, they likewise rule their relatives. It could be concluded that men could be women's freedoms as well as limitations towards their families. Men were rigorously bound to comply with specific traditions, practices, and rules made for women and young girls, as it were. Our general public plays a few parts, commitments, honors, relations, and customs just for women, since women think about a more fragile segment. Concerning women and young girls, our way of behaving is very discourteous. Men are intellectually and genuinely amazing, just men are better choices who effectively deal with their work and family. What effect of gender imbalance have on the two genders' well-being? In his research, he finds orientation imbalance causes medical problems for the two genders, like smoking issues, overweight, intellectual aggravation, misery, alcoholic propensities, and so on. As per the author, every one of the nations is completely centred around equal dispersion of pay and riches, equivalent open doors to representatives in the working environment, keeping the public authority guidelines and guidelines made by the public authority to support society, don't miss utilise the principal privileges, all ideas remembered for conduct orientation disparity ought to be decreased and controlled. The author's exploration incorporated the 10 nations with orientation imbalance listed by WHO districts. In the outcome, he discovered a few nations have the most elevated listed rates and the other nations have the least ordered rate. The principal purposes of the proficiency rate are neediness and expanding the rate of birth. For the most part, gender imbalances are worldwide issues. It's the distinction between men and women's business status in the working environment. In the research, the creator concludes that each nation should be centred on general wellbeing mediations and equivalent circulation of the financial assets of the general public to decrease orientation disparity.

Marilyn (1992) investigated the understudies' enduring gender inequality and furthermore confronted the manhandling in regards to their orientation in the professional college and universities. The research in ,this paper was directed at which types of orientation separation are looked at by understudies in universities and how they have honestly confronted segregation. Gender disparity hits the psychological place of understudies. Das substantial gender equity in work as well as considering different issues like early relationships, lowering baby death rates, and the improvement of wellbeing and training programs. Kyrö (2009) in this paper identifies the changes that occurred in the schooling system and how they are connected to different issues, including women's liberation. According to this study, women generally continue on to colleges for higher education. Yet, that doesn't mean we accomplished orientation uniformity. This paper depicts how much colleges actually accomplished in terms of change. Kersti (2019) in this paper learns about the beyond 10 years and depicts what orientation disparity puts a terrible mean on workers' presentation. Which steps were taken by the Korean government to decrease orientation preference in close work environments? The purpose of this study is to identify how to execute the regulations to eliminate or lessen gender inequality.

Joseph (2013) did an assessment on orientation inconsistency and put the centrality of sexual course detachment for ladies' encounters under crushing ceaselessly. Past evaluations have recommended that sexual heading generalising and different level-out elements might add to separation. At any rate, it isn't beyond a shadow of a doubt known how these fragments communicate with engaged sexual heading disengagement in typical working environments. The evaluations uncover how sexual bearing generalising converges in clear propensities with the orientation piece of work environments and moderate strategies, as frequently as conceivable through interactional parts of optional procedure use, to accomplish division. The disclosures propose the significance of social, aid, and interactional ramifications for orientation division.

Neitz (2016) in this paper, it's clear that improper ways of behaving is one of the most endemic sorts of violence against women and young women today. No matter how you look at its limitations all over the planet, unwanted sexual thoughts are an undeniable condition of work and preparation for a critical number of women and young women. The types of practises that cause it, as well as the nature and extent of the harm that it causes, differ by region, occupation, and control. It remains to be seen how seriously genuine complaints are taken, as well as the proportion of protection and remediation proposed to vary according to identity and affiliation. Globalisation has been a two-sided deal in the campaign to get women. As the world fights to persevere through the biggest monetary slump since the Remarkable Wretchedness, the overall release of business, likewise, informational entryways, will simply increase the number of women and young women feeble against an improper way of behaving. To adjust their little spending plans, states, chiefs, universities, and schools have recently begun to reduce or cut absolutely crucial resources for expectations and security.

Our general public is a male-ruled society, has all traditions, culture, and standards made against females. One common feature revealed in Haryana is the presence of a wide disparity in female labor. Analysts working on unique aberrations have harped on the expanding inclinations of disparity or intermingling, while practically every one of them noticed the commonness of imbalances just as its perseverance. In this case, advancement is thought to be impartial, and in this way, it is normal that females will profit alongside males from any improvement that happens. The acknowledgement that females should be explicitly tended to for their interests with the reproaching of the legend in regards to sexual equity/fairness, which involved analysts in the way of the majority in the hottest two decades, at last, came to be all the more generally recognised by the mid-nineties. Despite the fact that male and female forces have comparative characteristics, they are viewed as different because of their organic and physiological make-up.

Females have been put in a disadvantageous position as a result of sexual direction-related favouritism on a variety of grounds. For example, women don't have access to guidance, readiness, fitness progression, and basic administration in social, financial, and creative jobs, both on an individual and a social level. When women aren't given the chance to do important things in public life, progress is slowed down. This partition and monetary circumstance of females discuss sexual direction inclinations. Orientation balance in work power individuals' monetary viewpoints isn't simply a social or orientation equity issue and an extent of identical help; it is a critical piece of money-related progression. Irregularity in admittance to progress resources and in work openings among folks and females achieve a lower obligation to headway by females, who are half of the work power. As of not very far in the past, it was normal that improvement was physically unprejudiced that the two people and females could benefit much the same way from headway, and the upsides of progression mediations spread evenhandedly over the overall population, this has now exhibited to be a legend. The kept legacy of sexual direction divergence in all friendly orders over the world construes that there is no "level battleground. In our hustling lives, we will generally be speaking disregard that apparently the hugest grown-ups in our lives were our educators when we were growing up. It very well may be far from being plainly clear whether there is a lady behind an influential man, yet it is certain that there are a couple of exceptional teachers behind each useful man and lady. In learning, one can educate, and in setting you up to learn. Research finds teaching might be the best call in light of the following reasons: It is lying out and cutting down that offers an individual an opportunity to ceaselessly give signs of progress. It has its high concentrations and discouraged spots, yet as a rule, it's magnificent when you help youngsters with leaving school with better contrasted with normal evaluations and recognise they have a future. The children's energies; their advantage shows up and pushes them harder. Moreover, once in a while, these youngsters are genuinely fulfilled. It extends business opportunities' security. Without a doubt, even in the midst of monetary battles when different associations cut back, educators will be required.

Different organisations' jobs convey with them drawing in work and occasion plans. Above all else, get all gathering and open occasions off, which apparently will not be what is happening to accept you somehow sorted out some way to work in the secret district. Working in government moreover routinely guesses that you ought to be a piece of a connection, which can have a few damages, notwithstanding, encourage you to coordinate a reasonable pay and manages your tendencies.

Here recognising to get a handle on young Indian lady's characters is less to their objectives for higher degrees recorded as a hard copy. The investigation definite here is fundamental for a greater constant survey highlighted examining linkages between young women's capability practices in various lingos and their thoughts of self and character. The ladies' dissident techniques for unstructured start-to-finish gatherings maintained with a self-participatory procedure and part discernment were used to get the riches and simplicity of ladies' public and classified characters. Despite the hindrance shown by women to Western culture and methods of reasoning, they genuinely take on new subjectivities and positional ties as they will generally absorb the norms and values related. The greater receptiveness to an underpinning of high-level training opens up windows to the world, to Western methods of reasoning and world-view, joined with permission to the Internet, connect channels, insightful texts, books and magazines. As often as possible in conveying individual objectives that are contrary to their more traditional positions there is in like manner explicit security from this social assault; the ladies seem to project unquestionable cream characters that are dichotomous and conflictual.

All through the 1970s, and 1980s, issues connecting with women and aiding the least fortunate of the poor ruled improvement organisations, also the empty talk numerous offices enormous and little, public and private provided for program needs. Doubtlessly, native women are the least fortunate of poor people, among the planet's most un-addressed and the most taken advantage of women's situation in native social orders has not forever been great; there is not an obvious explanation to endeavour to paint it so. Contact by and mixing into the bigger monetary and political framework could really work on certain women's status, however, this isn't normally the situation. At the point when native social orders join bigger frameworks, this prompts a further masculinisation of governmental issues and incorporating these gatherings into other lawful customs frequently disintegrates women" customary privileges to land and assets.

Mental harassment by female partners is in like manner a reality. Fiscal self-sufficiency gives women more see in the overall population as observed by the working women. Working ladies feel they are standing up to more mental weight and despair than non-working women. Next no careful about acts and policies leaning toward ladies in the workplace. Clinical issues are furthermore a huge issue for working ladies. Working women have driven away from their little youths at home considering their work.

In literature dissected or conceptualised the psychosocial improvement of women, observational examinations of formative issues with every single female and material which investigated opportunities for future exploration and practice. Different and non-straight examples of improvement portrayed by discontinuities and times of security and progress are the standard for women; closeness and personality are the main points of interest all throughout women's lives, and the significance of connections and a feeling of connectedness to others are integral to the by and large formative interaction.

A load of Western European history conditions people to see human differentiations in childish protection from each other: dominating, subordinate, extraordinary, horrendous, up/down, predominant, and unsatisfactory. In an overall population where the extraordinary is portrayed to the extent that advantage rather than as a need might arise, there must continually be. Unacknowledged class contrasts keep ladies from getting each other's energy and innovative information. As of late, a women's magazine aggregate pursued the choice for one issue to print just exposition, it was a less "systematic" or "serious" work of art to say the verse. However, even the structure our inventiveness takes is much of the time a class issue. The writing of women of Variety is only sometimes remembered for women writing courses and never in other writing courses, nor in women's examinations in general. Again and again, the reason given is the writing on women of Variety must be shown. It's too challenging to even consider understanding.

Women were created through the ages, yet so far, most of the appropriate writers were men and the portrayal of ladies recorded as a hard copy was certainly uneven. A lot of it should be blamed on the way that in the old world, schooling was completely confined, and a large portion of individuals who could make was male. Nonetheless, the commitment of women to oral legends can't be underestimated – in society melodies, stories, verse and writing overall. This is a gander at the way women were depicted in writing through times. During the Victorian period, there was a ceaseless discussion over the jobs of women. While the period was overwhelmed by essayists who regarded women as other-worldly figures-honest, genuinely more fragile and nothing not as much as family items; women's privileges assembled a lot of consideration, women's liberation and females escaping their homes during the conflict times.

Christina Rossetti's 'Goblin Market' and Master Tennyson's "Lady of Shalott from the Victorians included a mission to achieve some higher information, which is restricted to men, and how, in their endeavour, they lose their capacity to return to the womanhood they were glad for. The Probationer, by AM Irvine, is the best illustration of the condition of women in the post-Victorian period. The novel also demonstrates the qualities of advanced women's rights by depicting a free and gifted female hero's professional and personal transition. Discussing the portrayal of women in Indian verse, it was political dissident, educationist, and lobbyist Mahadevi Verma who turned into the torchbearer of Hindi verse on women's issues. She additionally composed on issues of women's liberation and female sexuality, one that basically existed outside marriage. The incredible poetess drew motivation for her subjects from customary Hindu writing, which discussed freeing pictures.

Amrita Pritam ended up being one of the main voices in Indian territorial verse in the twentieth century. The author says about the Punjabi sections, which discussed the consequences of the India-Pakistan parcel in the district of Punjab and the women persecuted at the appointed time, that they achieved a faction status among verse sweethearts, and the late Kamala Das cleared the way for a deplorable style of women like confession booth verse, in which a typical subject was the investigation of the man-woman relationship. This style was therefore taken up by different female artists, like Gauri Deshpande and Chitra Narendran.

Additionally, Shobhaa De's audacious portrayal of women folk in her books. De's women range from customary, enslaved and minimized to incredibly current and freed women. De's books take a leaf from the metropolitan life and address a personal side of a metropolitan woman's life, likewise uncovering her predicament in present-day society. Likewise, fascinating is the manner in which she features a woman's part in the persecution and enduring of individual women, a viewpoint displayed in De's novel "Starry Nights." The women in De's books restore their lost fortunes, look exciting, change the standards, and are physically freed and nonconformist. As per Vinita Dawra Nangia, Scholarly Chief AutHer awards, "We are glad to share that more books by women's writers were shipped off to us for thought for this present year than in our past two versions of the women's writer awards." The AutHer awards anticipate empowering more women to put themselves out there through composition, and achieve a positive change in the fairly slanted orientation conditions in the distribution business. Here is a glance at the writers and their books that came to the waitlist under different classifications.

Conclusion

The status of Indian women has generally been centred on their pathetic condition of women. But it is also true that the status of women has improved over time, and it has also been seen to what extent women generally work in institutions and at home in a male-controlled society, and due to conservative thinking, women's participation has been ignored. Women tolerate sexual orientation harassment in their personal and professional lives, expressing dissatisfaction with it through inappropriate behavior, double standards of sexually intense quality, and abusive behaviour at home. However, there are massive contradictions between Indian and Western representations of women's emancipation. This paper proposes a non-discriminatory future for women's rights as a whole.

Works Cited

Paula Kyrö (2009). "Gender lenses identify different waves and ways of understanding women entrepreneurship." *Journal of Enterprising Culture* 17 (04), 393-418 (2009). https://www.worldscientific.com/doi/abs/10.1142/S021849580900045X.

Katz Marilyn (1992). Ideology and "The Status of women" in ancient Greece 21(4) *History and Feminist Theory* (Dec., 1992), https://doi.org/10.2307/2505416.

Cashdan Elizabeth (1995). "Hormones, Sex, and Status in Women." *Hormones and Behavior*, 29(3),354-366. https://science/article/abs/pii/S0018506X85710252.

Lerner Gerda (1969). *The lady and the mill girl: changes in the status of women in the age of Jackson,* 10(1), 5-15, https://www.jstor.org/stable/40640814.

"Effect of Gender Roles on Job Satisfaction: A Study on the Employees Working in Government Academic Sector in Haryana" in *International Journal of Entrepreneurial Research,* Volume 4, No.1, 2021/ Online ISSN: 2663-7588. Print ISSN: 2663-757X, Pages 1-3, Link: https://www.readersinsight.net/IJER/issue/current, Doi: 10.31580/ijer.v4i1.1561.

Yllo Kersti (2019). "Sexual Equality and Violence against Wives in American States." *Journal of Comparative Family Studies* , 14(1), 67-86.doi.org/10.3138/jcfs.14.1.67.

Joseph, C. (2013). "An analysis of the factors influencing the smallholder communal cotton farmers' decision to adopt contract farming – A case of Zaka district. Bull." *Environment Pharmacology. Life Science*, 2 (6): 131-134.

Jo Neitz (2016). "Humor, Hierarchy, and the Changing Status of Women." *Interpersonal and Biological Process*, 43(3), 211223.Doi/10.1080/00332747.1980.11024068?journalCode=upsy20.

McAuslan, P. (2004). "Sexual assault and alcohol consumption: What do we know about their relationship and what types of research are still needed?" *Aggression and Violent Behavior,* 9, 271-303. Doi:10.1016/S1359-1789(03)00011-9.

List of Contributors

1. **Shikha Sharma**, Ph.D Research Scholar, Department of English, B.P.S.M.V Khanpur Kalan, Sonipat Haryana.
2. **Bhairab Barman**, Ph.D Research Scholar, Dept. of Humanities and Social Sciences, IIT Jodhpur, India.
3. **Manidip Chakraborty**, Assistant Professor, Dept. of English, Bhairab Ganguly College, Kolkata.
4. **Dr. Kailash Kumar**, Assistant Professor, Dept. of English, Wangcha Rajkumar Government College, Arunachal Pradesh.
5. **Dr. Priya Raghav**, Associate Professor, Department of English, Lingaya's Vidyapeeth
6. **Ms. Sarita**, Assistant Professor, Department of Psychology, Lingaya's Vidyapeeth
7. **Dr. Sonali Mahanta**, Ph.D, Jawaharlal Nehru University, New Delhi.
8. **Dr. B.Chandana**, Assistant Professor, Dept. of English, Matrusri Engineering College, Hyderabad.
9. **Dr. Salma Javed**, Ph.D, Aligarh Muslim University, Uttar Pradesh, India.
10. **Dr. Smritikana Ghosh**, Assistant Professor, Radha Govind University
11. **Shrishti Dey**, Lecturer, Gurukul Global Academy, Assam
12. **Akhila Ajith**, PostGraduate Student, Sree Sankaracharya University of Sanskrit, Kalady.
13. **Apoorva Poonia**, Ph.D Research Scholar, Department of English, Chaudhary Devi Lal University, Sirsa.
14. **Jagari Mukherjee**, Research Scholar, Seacom Skills University, West Bengal

15. **Biju Chetia & Daisy Priya Gogoi**, Assistant Professor, Dept. of English, Khowang College, Assam
16. **Dr. Nivedita Gupta**, Assistant Professor, Dept. of English, Amity University, Noida.
17. **Dr. Gurpreet Kour**, Associate Professor, Department of Linguistics (English), Dr. C. V. Raman University, Bilaspur (C.G)
18. **Hina Koser**, Guest Lecturer, C.C.S University Meerut
19. **Hiba Khan**, Post Graduation Student, C.C.S University Meerut.
20. **Supriyo Mapder**, Postgraduation Student, Department of English, Presidency University.
21. **Ms. Suparna Roy**, Postgraduation English, B.Ed Student, Central Modern College of Education, Kolkata.
22. **Nahan N. K.**, M. A English Student, Noble Women's College, Malappuram.
23. **Deepa Sharma**, Assistant Professor, Maharishi Markandeshwar (deemed to be University) Ambala.

Index